DODGING MINES IN THE MINEFIELD OF LIFE

How I Survived Religion, Booze,
Romance and the Music Industry

Jim Hoffine

Dare Publications
jimhoffine@aol.com
darepublications@gmail.com
Birmingham, AL

Dodging Mines in the Minefield of Life
How I Survived Religion, Booze, Romance, and the Music Business

Copyright © 2019 by Jim Hoffine

All rights reserved. This book or any portion thereof may not be reproduced or used in any manner whatsoever without the express written permission of the publisher except for the use of brief quotations in a book review.

Printed in the United States of America
First Printing, 2019
ISBN 978-0-9916508-2-8

To Dalton and Brooke,

The Best Children A Dad Could Ever Ask For

Acknowledgment

Once again, I would like to acknowledge the tireless efforts of Martha Williams, who edited this manuscript for both grammar and content. She is the smartest English teacher I know, besides being a good friend. She edited my first book and lived to tell about it. Any remaining errors the reader might find here are likely due to my altering the manuscript after her editing.

Table of Contents

Introduction 1
Chapter One: Showing Up 3
Chapter Two: From New Orleans to Birmingham 9
Chapter Three: Early Steps into the Minefield 17
Chapter Four: My Parents 25
Chapter Five: High School Days 33
Chapter Six: The Summer of Love 43
Chapter Seven: Saved! 51
Chapter Eight: Off to Grad School 59
Chapter Nine: A Short Stint in Michigan 69
Chapter Ten: Headfirst into the Lounge Circuit 73
Chapter Eleven: Twenty Years as a Keyboard Warrior 79
Chapter Twelve: Getting a "Real Job" 91
Chapter Thirteen: Breaking the Chains of Religious Dogma, Finally ... 97
Chapter Fourteen: Watch Out for Romance!!!! 103
Chapter Fifteen: Beware the Booze Mine!!! 113
Chapter Sixteen: Watch Out for the Religion Mine!!! 121
Chapter Seventeen: Final Thoughts 131

Introduction

"Man is born to trouble, as surely as sparks fly upward," quipped Job's fair-weather friend Eliphaz towards the beginning of that ancient legend in the Bible. And he was surely right about *that*, despite saying some other pretty crazy things.

Trouble visits us all from the moment of our birth, though the level of troubles we experience can be vastly different. If we are born into an industrialized nation with a decent economy, stable government, and democratized ideals, then our troubles are likely to generally be less than those of someone born into a poor country or a failed state. Of course, being born into poverty or as a member of a minority race will, even in our relatively wealthy society, raise your chances of encountering trouble.

But one thing is sure: Regardless of the circumstances of your birth, troubles are going to visit you during your lifetime. Certain of these troubles are inescapable, such as illness, emotional pain, death, disappointment, and the like. Others are partially or fully self-inflicted, and it is these that are foremost in my mind when I think of "life as a minefield."

Of course, the metaphor of life as a minefield is not a perfect one. Usually, if you step on a mine in the physical world, you don't survive the experience. So maybe a better way to picture the metaphor is to treat it like a minefield *in a video game*. In a few of those games, you can step on a mine, get shot, or get harpooned by an opponent, *yet still survive the ordeal*. You just reconstitute yourself in some way and continue with the battle.

And this is what occurred with me in my encounters with religion, romance, booze, and my occupation as a lounge musician. Any one of these things could have killed me, and once or twice almost did. But I recovered from them all, and today my life is one of general stability, contentment, and optimism. I realize that my experiences with these things are not going to match perfectly with every reader's personal experiences, but I suspect that some or even many of them will be similar.

I also realize that there are yet chapters of my life to be written, and that the unforeseen can pose new challenges to successful living. But as far as these particular minefield obstacles are concerned, I have stepped on them all and lived to tell about it. And I am now much better equipped to avoid them altogether, at least in their more dangerous forms.

It seemed to me that the best way to approach this recitation of my life adventure was to start at the beginning, hit the highlights (or lowlights) of my journey, and then spend the final chapters sharing my take on how to navigate through these minefields of life.

Life is good, and can be even better, and to the extent that any of my readers gain tools to help with navigating through their own challenges in life, my goal will have been accomplished.

Jim Hoffine, Birmingham, AL
August 2019

Chapter One
SHOWING UP

Comedian and film maker Woody Allen is cited as saying, "80% of life is just *showing up*." And that I did, at daybreak on a date in the middle of January, 1952, in Kansas City, Missouri. I had no control over the date, time, or the event itself, but there I was. I was born with the moniker "George Kirk" to a very young and unwed woman who reportedly had a romantic *tete-a-tete* with an American soldier. Rather than suffer the shame concurrent with the times, or the economic hardship of raising a child as a single mother, she put me up for adoption. A short six weeks later, I was adopted by a couple who were physically unable to have children of their own. Three years earlier they had adopted my sister Jane, and they wanted a boy to complete the duo.

My luck in this scenario was profound, in the sense that my adoptive parents *desperately wanted me and my sister* more than anything else in life. And it showed throughout my time with them on this planet. I always felt loved and needed by my new parents, and a bonus feature was that they loved and needed each other. There was lots of love in that house from the very get-go.

Of course, the first order of business after my birth was to rename me, and I went from being "George Kirk" to being named "James Edward Hoffine." The intent was to call me "Jimmy," and that's how it was from then on. The hospital nurse reportedly remarked that I looked like a "Jimmy" much more than a "George," perhaps because even as a baby I had a happy, goofy grin on my face. Who knows, but I feel better as a "Jimmy" or (now) "Jim" than I think I would have as a "George." (My apologizes to George Harrison, George Clooney, George Washington, George Michael, and all the other accomplished and honorable "Georges" throughout history).

Off to "The Big Easy"

Just a year after my birth, my family moved to New Orleans, LA to open a business. My dad had graduated from the University of Kansas with a business degree, and he opened a greeting card and novelty shop in the downtown New Orleans area. It was quite successful, and our life on Ridgewood Drive in suburban Metairie was the stuff of the American Dream: Upper middle-class trappings, good schools, close-knit community life, and pretty much everything one might hope for. I'm sure my parents were acutely aware of their fortunate lot, as they both were children of German immigrants who fled the impending Nazi crisis in Germany in the early Twentieth Century.

While I was a toddler, my parents would occasionally—but only occasionally—take my sister and me to an A&W Root Beer stand just across a main thoroughfare from our home. My first encounter with that root beer was nearly life-altering, as I had never tasted anything quite so wonderful—what with the fizziness and the sweet bark-root flavor. So around the age of five, I began to ask my Mother if I could walk across the road and get a root beer on my own. "Absolutely not," she warned, "that highway is dangerous!" The road to which she referred was The Airline Highway, a busy thoroughfare separating our house from the A&W. "You can cross that road when you're *seven*, but not until," she added.

Now, to a five-year-old, the span between five and seven years of age is *an eternity*, and it passed painfully slowly. But eventually my seventh birthday came around, and I reminded her of her promise. "Oh, alright," she conceded, and after sponging a quarter from her and, after sponging a quarter from her, I set out for my coveted birthday present. That was maybe the best root beer I have ever experienced.

Climbing Poles and Walking on The Moon

Yet another recollection I have from this same general time period has to do with the high school in the area (Metairie High), which was closely adjacent to our house—being literally separated from us by a single home. The school was a source of fascination to me, with its winding concrete paths, spooky looking structures (to a five-year-old), and massive playground. And positioned over most of the sidewalks outside the classroom buildings were flat, shed-type roof covers, attached to very climbable metal poles on each side. Of course, these poles were entirely too great a temptation to my neighborhood friends and me; and we would shimmy up them and walk back and forth on the flat roofing as if we were walking on the moon.

One day, not long after we had begun our near-daily afternoon trespassing on school grounds, three kitchen ladies exited their building at a dead run, waving their arms frantically and shouting at us, "You kids get out of here! Get on home, now!!" We immediately shimmied down the poles, hit the sidewalk, and ran frantically to our respective houses. It scared us so bad that we cried all the way home, and naturally I confessed all that had happened to my alarmed Mother. She was great about the whole affair, even going next door to speak with the ladies who had caused our trauma. I imagine she played both ends of the issue, apologizing for our errant behavior, while at the same time requesting that they not scare the bejesus out of her son and his friends. She was a peacemaker like that.

The French Quarter and the Docks

Other related memories from this early life period include my parents taking my sister and me to *The Blue Room* in the French Quarter for our birthdays (and there treating us to our first stage show), getting a charcoal portrait done of us in Pirate's Alley, those ridiculously succulent French Quarter pastries (Beignets), and taking us to the docks to see the massive tankers tied up just twenty feet away from where we stood. It was on those docks I developed what is called *megalophobia*, or "the fear of large objects." This same fear also visited me the first time I ever set foot in New York City, where the towering seventy- and eighty-story skyscrapers on both sides of the street freaked me out. I have since gotten over this fear to a large degree, although I'm not sure how I did it. Perhaps realizing that fearing inanimate objects is completely silly is what accounts for my cure, but I don't know.

Coffee, with Chickory

Around that time my Mother also introduced me to a vice that has followed me down to the present day: *coffee*. It's not really a vice, of course, but I may have been a bit young to jump on that particular wagon of liquid stimulus. And I remember just how it happened. We had a neighbor a couple of blocks over named Mrs. Mertz, a smallish woman with a thick Cajun accent, and she was well-known for brewing some of the tastiest (and lethal) coffee in our community. It wasn't just coffee; it was coffee *with Chicory*. If you've never tasted that particular concoction before, think of it this way: It's very much like your normal everyday coffee brewed very strongly, but with a mule-sized "kick" to it. Heady stuff, indeed. Of course, when we moved away from Louisiana, we began drinking regular non-Chicoried coffee, and later in life I had to switch to decaf due to my inherent physical aversion to caffeine. But coffee is a life necessity that I will never abandon, thanks to Mrs. Mertz and my mom, even if the Surgeon General comes out with scientific evidence that it can cause the growth of a third eye or an eleventh toe.

Playing in the Fog

One other fond memory I have of my life in New Orleans has to do with the mosquito trucks that roamed the streets of our neighborhood in the summer. These trucks were equipped with rear-mounted gizmos of some sort that sprayed a thick white cloud of mosquito-killing gas, an absolute necessity in the unbelievably hot and humid climate that bred the little buggers *en masse*. We would run out into the street and get directly behind these trucks, engulfing ourselves in the thick white cloud of this pesticide, not being able to see anything at all in any direction. This was fun for us, and part of the wonder of discovering life. I am stunned that I still have functioning lungs after that display of unbridled stupidity, but evidently Mother Nature gave me a strong set of breathers.

Our family left New Orleans when I was almost eight years old, and I was still a good ways away from encountering any of the true minefields in my life. Life—up to this point—was pretty much a Shangri-La, a virtual fairy tale of a loving family closely bound and navigating the 1950s together.

Chapter Two
FROM NEW ORLEANS TO BIRMINGHAM

Around the time I was seven, something happened that did not fit with my perception of *life as Shangri-La*. One weekday afternoon, my mother and I were in our garage as she was doing laundry, and my uncle's family drove up in their car. It was *mid*-afternoon, so this was highly unusual. My father's brother, Lyman, had moved to New Orleans to help him start the new greeting card business, and ordinarily he would have been at work. So seeing their car drive up at that hour was very strange, and my mother and I did not know that he had taken the day off to take his sons to Lake Pontchartrain for an afternoon of swimming.

As my aunt and her sons exited the car and came walking up to the open garage door, my aunt blurted out, "Lyman is dead! He drowned in Pontchartrain, trying to save Bobby and Dickie." (His sons). When I first heard that, I laughed. I thought they were joking. After all, life was Shangri-La, and death was not possible in that world. But they were *not* joking, and after a few minutes I realized the ugly reality of what they were saying. It was the first time I had been confronted with the notion that really bad things can and do happen in life.

My mother immediately called my dad, and he was home within minutes. After a good deal of crying and hugging, we all ended up in my parents' bedroom on our knees around the bed, praying for strength to survive this horror.

Apparently, Bobby and Dickie had been swimming in the lake, got a little too far out, and began to be sucked down by the undercurrent.

Lyman swam out to save them and was successful in the attempt. They all three made it back to shore, but apparently my uncle had swallowed a good deal of water and strained his heart to the point where it gave out. He died on the beach. We later discovered that the Hoffine family has a history of heart disease, as both my grandfather and my father had heart attacks in subsequent years.

In the months that followed, my dad kept the business going, and Aunt Monnie (Lyman's wife) did what she could to help him. However, she felt that my dad was not being fair to her in the administration of the business (at least, that's how I remember it), and she wanted to buy him out. He was a kind man, and he accepted her proposal. This meant, of course, that he forfeited his entire stake in the business that he had mostly built, and he began searching for a new place to open up a new greeting card business.

And that's how we ended up in Birmingham, Alabama. Starting from scratch, my dad opened "Deluxe Greeting Cards and Novelties" on 5th Ave. North and 18th St. in the heart of the city, and we purchased a home in the wealthy suburb of Vestavia Hills.

<u>New City, New Culture</u>

Although New Orleans and Birmingham are both cities in what is geographically considered "The South," the inherent culture of both is somewhat different. New Orleans is more cosmopolitan, an ethnic melting pot, while Birmingham is more of a rural culture gone urban. By that I mean that the ugliness of racial discrimination and "classism" is more evident than one would find in The Big Easy (at least among the rank and file New Orleanians).

And things for me didn't start out as well as I had hoped. I was enrolled in the second grade at Vestavia Hills Grammar School, and my fellow male classmates were more sports oriented than I was. Now, I loved sports, and my dad had turned me into a very competent baseball player, but I was smaller in frame than my counterparts in the neighborhood and in school generally.

This was not a really big deal until around the fifth grade, when my diminutive frame began to be much smaller by comparison than those of the other guys in my class (the onset of puberty). This caused me a good deal of pain, in the sense that being smaller made me less efficient in sports and less attractive to my female classmates (in whom I was just beginning to develop a serious interest).

I remember one afternoon, after being rejected in a neighborhood football game because I was too "bony," I sat down at dusk on the brick stoop near the lower back door of our house, and just started bawling. I was hurt, because I craved the acceptance of my neighborhood mates, and they had brutally rejected me.

The Piano To The Rescue

From the earliest time I could remember, my family had an old upright piano in the house. I was fascinated by it, especially when my dad would sit down and play "The Church in the Wildwood" on it. He did a pretty good job of it, despite the fact that he had blown off three and a half fingers on his left hand in a shotgun accident when he was fourteen. That piano was always beckoning to me to come and bang on its keys, even though I had no ability to make anything close to what might resemble music on it.

So from about the time I was five until I was seven I would constantly just bang on those black and white objects of my fascination, much to the chagrin of the others in the house. In fact, my clanging around on the piano earned me an ultimatum from my parents: "Either take lessons and learn how to make something that sounds like music on it, or we're getting rid of it!" This demand intrigued me greatly, and I willingly agreed to do just that.

My mom then got me into weekly instruction with a sweet little German lady named Mrs. Kroh. I was just seven years old, but Mrs. Kroh was an able teacher, and she started me out by teaching me how to read music. From the very first lesson I KNEW this was what I wanted to do in life. The mechanics of it all came easily to me, and being able to make the piano sound like anything other than cats screwing was magical to me. No one had to coerce me to practice; I was obsessed with it. My usual routine each day after school was to come home, have a bite to eat, and then sit at the piano practicing for two or three hours until dinner. However, all of a sudden the complaints surfaced again, but this time for a different reason. I was actually playing music instead of producing headache-inducing noise, but I was doing it *all the time*. I guess too much of a good thing was perceived of as a bad thing. Yet they encouraged me to continue with the lessons, and I ended up studying classical music for the next ten years.

The point here is that, while I was not as big and brawny as my contemporaries, I could do something they could not. And they respected the fact that I could play as well as I did, because they also were interested in music. In short, *the piano had come to my emotional rescue.*

This was the beginning of my lifelong relationship with playing music, and it led me to all kinds of different places, some for better and some for worse. The first mine in life's minefield was approaching.

From Classical Music to the "Devil's Racket"

Mrs. Kroh realized that I was a natural at music, and she used to brag that I was "the next Liberace." (Liberace, for those of you who may not know, was a famous classical-turned-pop entertainer of the 1950s-80s. His name became synonymous with great piano playing worldwide, although there were other serious concert pianists who were his superior. Still, he was a serious and accomplished classical pianist, but at some point he figured out he could make a lot more money in music with a flashy show that featured popular tunes of the day. And he made a LOT of money at it).

At some point after three years under Ms. Kroh's tutelage, she told my parents that she had taken me as far as she was able to take me. She recommended that they put me in the preparatory department at Samford University (that's "Samford," not "Stanford"), a local college that had a very respected music department. They did so, and at age ten I was studying with a very accomplished professor of music on a college campus. I went on to study an additional seven years there, and during that time I won and placed in a number of state piano competitions.

However, at some point around age twelve, another musical influence began to catch my attention—*rock and roll*. I had discovered pop music on AM radio, and suddenly my love of classical music started to take a second place to the fabulous new sounds of Chuck Berry, The Beatles, and The Rolling Stones. This disturbed my mother, I think, but she never made much of it to me. And I'm grateful she didn't. This new influence would shape much of what I've done in my life, and along with religion and academics, formed the three dominant interests and drivers of my existence. To this day these three things still motivate much of what I spend my time doing.

Since it was at this time that I also began to be interested in girls, I tried to display my piano-playing talents to them whenever I could. My thinking was, "I might not be as big and muscular as the other guys, but I can do *this*." And it worked to some degree, but something was missing. I noticed that every time I watched a band on TV or heard one live, the girls were always ogling *the guitar player*. And right then and there I learned a cardinal truth about being a musician: *Girls like guitar players better than piano or keyboard players.* And that's been true throughout my career as a musician.

So I thought to myself, "Alright, damn it. I'm going to learn how to play the guitar." And I did. My sister had been given an inexpensive *Stella* guitar around that time, but she really didn't have much interest in it. So I took that guitar, and her beginner's guitar book, and sat down on the front steps of our house in Vestavia. I opened the book to one of the first songs listed, and discovered how to place my fingers on the frets to play different chords. I mastered a simple fret fingering of the C, F, and G chords, and within about ten minutes I was singing along to "The Ballad of Jesse James." And although I still loved playing the piano, playing the guitar became an equally powerful interest.

I was so excited about being able to play the guitar that I practiced all the time, along with practicing the piano. I mowed a few yards and scraped together twenty bucks, and a junior high school chum sold me his Sears *Silvertone* beginner electric guitar. The sound of it was bordering on atrocious, and its appearance was even more atrocious: it was turquoise with a white pick guard! But I loved it, polishing it regularly and keeping new strings on it.

I became good enough about a year later to gain an audition with a band whose members were older Berry High School students (red flag), and I got the job as rhythm guitar player. I was psyched beyond belief! And when the time came around to play our first gig together, I was beside myself. It happened on a Saturday afternoon in the rec room of our keyboard player's parents' house, and the audience was a bunch of his dad's rich friends. They were there for some social function, and were of course "old" people, but it didn't matter. I got to play my first gig in a real band, and I felt like a rock star. We played for about two hours, I think, and when it was over I knew that I wanted to be a guitar player for the rest of my life. Yes, this rock band life was for me!!! And it led me to some places that nearly killed me.

Girls, Girls, Girls

I loved both grammar school and junior high school in many ways, and learning about math tables and the history of my state—particularly the Native American tribes who were responsible for much of the current geographical and architectural nomenclature contained in it—was never a chore to me. I loved to read and learn new things, and I developed many interests due to my inherently inquisitive nature.

But it was right around the tender age of ten that I discovered another strong interest: Girls! I would say that the fourth grade was pivotal for this interest, 'cause it was the first time I discovered what it felt like to have a "girlfriend." Her name was Jennie Gray, and she was the prototype of almost every girl I have been attracted to until this very day—long black hair, olive-colored skin, ruby-colored lips, and a smile that went on for days. Her teeth were the whitest of white, and she was tall and thin. Tall, yes, though not taller than I was. I don't think she'd mind me discussing her in these pages, 'cause I have nothing but very positive things to say about her. Plus, she moved far away when I was about fourteen, and I never saw her again.

The first "romantically" social contact I had with Jennie came during Valentine's Day around 1962. We fourth graders were tasked by our teacher with making homemade Valentine's Day cards, and of course I had to have someone to address the card to. The choice, for me, was a no brainer—*Jennie*! But I was scared shitless, 'cause this was all new to me. What if she said "no" to the "Will You Be My Valentine" message prominently plastered all over the front of my card? I would be crushed! But she thankfully said "yes," and as much as a 10-year-old can be in love, I was. I was thrilled, although she never was interested in any of the usual physical manifestations of such a "serious" relationship—no hugs, no kisses, no holding hands. And frankly, neither was I. We were ten years old, for Chrissake!

I also remember begging my parents to take her and me to a movie at the new theater downtown which featured what was called "Cinerama." It was a regular movie screen, but it was slightly curved in concave fashion. That was supposed to make the viewer's experience more life-like, or something like that. It was a long way from today's I-Max and Dolby sound-based theatres, to be sure, but nonetheless a slight advance in cinematic technology. I just knew she'd be *so* impressed if I took her there on a date, and that it would make her like me even more. But alas, my parents said "NO, you're only in the fourth grade!" And I was disappointed. But it was just as well, 'cause not long after that Jennie dumped me for a fifth grader who was bigger, taller, and more muscular than myself. "Ah, love lost, and at such a tender age." But I got over it in just a few days, and I soon had my sights set on another female classmate.

Of course, all this romantic silliness occurred before my body had gone through "the change," which for me happened in the sixth grade. Now *that* was something, and in the earliest days of it I didn't have a clue about what the Hell was going on with me. My father had passed away when I was in the fifth grade, so he wasn't around to explain the physiological basics to me. Eventually, I asked my poor mother to tell me about it and, bless her sweet heart, she fumbled through a very basic and awkward explanation of "what goes where," and how "after a certain number of months a baby comes out." She did her very best, but it took learning it from my school peers in later months to get much of a grasp of the details. And frankly, they didn't have it quite right, either. But, as all of us eventually did, I learned the complexities of the sexual nature of human beings. And then, so to speak, "it was on!" Girls, romance, sex, and all related things occupied a good deal of my thoughts when I was awake. And again, another component of the looming mines in the minefield of my life had manifested itself.

Chapter Three
EARLY STEPS INTO THE MINEFIELD

One of the passions of my early developmental years was baseball. I had watched the pros on TV quite a lot, and when my dad asked at me at age 9 if I'd like to learn how to pitch, I was thrilled. So for the next year we ventured into our back yard and he taught me the basics. He had a catcher's mitt, I had a regular glove, and he sat behind a 2" X 4" piece of wood he had cut to the same width as a home plate. He taught me how to throw a curve, a drop, and a knuckleball with some precision. I didn't have much of a fastball, though, given my bony frame and lack of definable muscles.

    At the same time, he had volunteered to be a coach in the Vestavia Little League, and of course I was always on his team (as was the local custom). I pitched and played second base during those 3 short years before his sudden death, and I continued to play under other coaches for a couple of years after that. One of those coaches—another "Jimmy" as I recall—was a young 20-something fellow who had a great natural comradery with us youngsters. One day at practice, he asked if we'd like to attend a pool party on Friday night at one of the team mothers' home. "There'll be girls there," he said, and he needed to say no more. We were all thirteen to fourteen years old, armed with burgeoning hormones, and we couldn't wait to get to that party. The time arrived and we piled out of the transport vehicles and gathered around the pool in the rear of the residence. I don't quite remember when, or how, but one of the girls there in that rather large bunch took a liking to me. Her name was "Mary Jane (something)," and she was thirteen, like me. I was quite attracted to her (she was a brunette), and she seemed fun. We talked a lot, and when the night came to a close she asked if she could come over to my house some time. "Yes, please," I said, and about a week later her mom brought her over to our house in Vestavia. She dropped her off, and Mary Jane and I went down into our basement so we could be alone.

You have to understand that I was as "green" as green could be when it came to the female gender, and I had never even kissed one of them. So we sat around on a couch for a couple of hours doing not much of anything at all. She put her arm around me (I think she was ahead of me in the *boy-girl touching department*), and I was scared shitless. Much later in my life I realized that she was waiting for me to kiss her, but I just sat there like a *schmoe*. The time passed painfully slow, and I'm pretty sure she was thinking "What's wrong with this guy? Is he too wimpy to kiss me?" But she was polite, and when she left she told me she was going to Florida to live with her grandmother for the summer. I said, "OK, but I'll write you every day!" and I called her the next day to get her Florida address (no cell phones or internet in those days). I was smitten, and I wrote her every day and even sent her a gift or two from the shipping department of our family business.

Around mid-summer our family took a weekend trip to Panama City, Florida, and I was excited because mom had told me I could call Mary Jane long distance from our motel. I was buzzing with anticipation 'cause I REALLY liked this girl. When we got settled into the motel, I went into the bedroom and called her from the phone. "Hello," she said, and I replied "Hi, Mary Jane. It's Jimmy!! Did you get my letters and the gifts I sent?" "Yes," she said, but in her voice I could tell something was wrong. She explained, "Look, Jimmy, you're a nice guy and all, but I have a new boyfriend here. I don't 'like' you anymore."

And it was at that very moment that I, for the very first time in my life, experienced the terrible feeling of romantic rejection. It was love spurned.

I had stepped on a mine, and it exploded with great force. I had experienced the rejection of friends before, and the disappointment of important plans being suddenly cancelled, but this was something entirely different. It hurt—with a kind of hurt I had never experienced before—and I felt like a ton of bricks had been dropped on me. I said "Bye" to her, hung up the phone, and immediately walked out on the beach. It was about 8 o'clock at night, and the beach was deserted, save for a couple of people a few hundred yards away. The moon was shining bright, illuminating the incoming waves as they melted into the shore. And I wept. I didn't know what this terrible feeling was that had suddenly assaulted me, but I knew it was something I didn't ever want to experience again. Of course, this wasn't the last time in my life I would experience romantic rejection, but in my later years I was more emotionally equipped to handle it.

Mine Number Two — "The Demon Rum"

It was around the same time during my thirteenth year that I discovered yet another explosive device lurking in life's soil: "demon rum," as alcohol was dubbed during Prohibition. The crowd that I was running with in junior high was a little wilder than your average Joes were, and at this young age we thought that booze was a really cool thing. We couldn't legally buy it, obviously, and that made it all the more attractive to us. Plus our older peers swore by it, leaving a lot of us to envision it as a rite of passage into manhood.

It seems that one of my classmates at Berry had overheard one of the older boys talking about a quart of Scotch whiskey that he had hidden in the crawl space beneath some other student's house. I don't recall the details of my thought process, but my immediate response to hearing about it was to plan a heist of that highly sought-after bottle of fun. So the next afternoon, as I was walking home from school, I took a slight detour and approached the house where the beverage bottle lay waiting for me. I cut through the yard and spied the wooden access door in the stone foundation block. I was pleased to see the door had no lock on it, and in less than five seconds I opened it, grabbed the hooch, and took off running. I really don't think I was inclined towards thievery as a thirteen-year-old, but this was *booze! Hooch! Firewater!*

When I got home with the spoil, I hid it in my closet and went next door to announce my theft to my neighbor and best friend Sam. Sam was my same age, and our level of inquisitiveness about hitherto unexperienced things in life was very similar. This is how the conversation went:

Me: *"Hey, man. Guess what I got?"*
Sam: *"What?"*
Me: *"A bottle of booze."*
Sam: *"Really?"*
Me: *"Yeah, really. Wanna come over tomorrow afternoon and help me drink it?"*
Sam: *"Sure. I'll be there."*

Now, I had never had a single drop of alcohol pass through my lips up to that point in life. I was totally ignorant of how to drink it, what it would do to me, or what the aftermath of drinking it would be like. All I knew was that this was "it"—the pathway to manhood, coolness, and boundless fun. So when Sam arrived that next afternoon just after school, I showed him the bottle and we sat down to begin our adventure. As I recall, we poured a little into a couple of glasses and took a sip. "Arghhhh," I thought, "that tastes really bad!" So I thought, "Maybe we should mix a little Seven-Up in with it to make it tolerable." And we did.

A couple of hours later, I woke up in my bed, stark naked, with my visiting grandparents looking down at me, disgusted. I looked down over the bed, and there was a half-eaten cheese sandwich, and what looked to be a small pile of somebody's vomit adjacent to it. Sam was gone, evidently back to his house, and my grandparents began to question me about what the Hell was going on. It seems I had drunk a couple of glasses of "Scotch and Seven," eaten part of a sandwich, barfed, ripped off my clothes, and passed out. There wasn't much I could do to spin these events in a positive way to my horrified grandparents, so I just looked sheepish and prayed they wouldn't tell my mother when she got home from work. If I remember correctly, they didn't, and I went to bed early and hoped this sense of shame and physical pain I was in would disappear before I had to get up and go to school the next morning.

And thus was my introduction to booze—a land mine I would stumble over many subsequent times in life. And rather than being the fabulous fun-filled "ride at the fair" that I expected, it turned out to be an unpleasant ride that led to puking, getting naked, embarrassing myself, and a feeling that I had been run over by an eighteen-wheeler.

California: Surfing, Sex, and Rock'N'Roll

About a year later, when I was fourteen, my mother decided the family should take a trip to California to visit my (maternal) uncle, "Uncle Loren." He lived in Oakland, just across the bay from San Francisco. I was pretty psyched about it, as I envisioned California as a "Mecca" of sun, rock'n'roll music, surfing, and girls—all being things that formed the focus of my life.

So we piled into our 1963 Chevy Biscayne—me, my mother, and my sister—and we set out at 6 AM one bright summer morning. (Flying as a mode of transportation was not as common as it is now, as it was expensive, and would've left us with no affordable means of transportation once we got there.) The trip was over two thousand miles in length, and required about three days on the road. It was July—a sweltering July—and we crossed the desert out West in that rolling automotive hunk of metal with *no air conditioner* on board. Air conditioning in cars was nowhere near as common as it is now (are there *any* cars sold without it these days?), and it was 118 degrees in Needles, CA when we arrived. We had tried to improvise an air conditioner somewhere in Arizona by filling a plastic dish tub with ice and positioning it under the front air vents in the Chevy's floorboard walls. But that was a futile endeavor, and we nearly died of heat exhaustion on the way.

But we eventually got to Uncle Loren's apartment in Oakland, and we began our two-week sightseeing journey from north to south in the Golden State. Notable stops were in San Francisco (a gorgeous *collage* of beautiful landscaping, architecture, rolling hills, and Fisherman's Wharf), Sacramento (the Capital), Pismo Beach (where I rented, and was twice assaulted by, a surfboard three times my size), and finally Los Angeles. While we were in Los Angeles, we drove thirty minutes south to Anaheim where Disneyland is located. There's one thing that I remember vividly from Mouse-Land, and that was the band that was playing on one of the stages there. I don't remember the name of the band, but they were fantastic. They had a wall of *Fender* amps (which I was drooling over, since I couldn't even begin to afford one), and every one of them was playing a *Fender* guitar (which I also could not afford). This experience solidified in me what I had always wanted to do: play in a rock'n'roll band. And there I was, in the clean California air and sun, watching a surf-music-oriented band play as the dusk descended. It was magical, and would influence what I would do in the years to come.

Of course, every beach we visited while on the left coast was populated by bikini-clad girls sporting deep tans. As a recent adolescent, I was a little more than titillated by the experience. This was amplified by interaction with my (not-by-birth) cousin Eva, a California native who traveled around Los Angeles with us. She was a year older than I was, and fairly attractive to me, and we sort of hit it off. She had told me in private about a couple of sexual experiences she had engaged in, and I was more than a little intrigued. I sincerely think she was offering to "de-flower" me, but I was still scared shitless of such a thing, and the farthest we went was a little hand-holding in the back seat of our car which was filled with the family's adults. I look back at that and laugh at how green I was at this juncture of life, but I would certainly "make up for it" later on. (I did mention that I was not related to her by birth, right? I mean, I lived a great deal of my life in Alabama, but we weren't *those* kind of Alabamians!)

I only bring up this excursion to California because it was a cultural catalyst for some of the things that would become the land mines in my life: Romance/sex, playing music professionally, and the party culture.

Chapter Four
MY PARENTS

Before I go any farther in this recitation of my survival through life's minefield, I'd like to insert a parenthesis about my parents. I believe that if I had not had the type of early upbringing I had, I might have had a much harder time surviving the mines that I stepped on. A great many of my friends and acquaintances were not as fortunate as I was when it came to the families they were born into, and many of them struggled mightily because of it. Some even died from their mine encounters.

When it came to the parent "lottery," I hit the bloody jackpot. Yeah, I was one lucky son of a gun. My dad was the son of a Kansas farm boy of German heritage, and my mom was the daughter of German refugees from World War 1. They met in Enterprise, Kansas, a small town just outside of Abilene, the capitol. After a fairly typical courtship they married and set out to start a family. But after a number of years of trying, they were told by the local medical establishment that it would be a physical impossibility for them to have children.

So they purposed to adopt children, and in their early and mid-thirties they were successful. They adopted my sister Jane first, then nearly three years later adopted me (from different birth parents). I was adopted at around the age of six weeks, and the same was true for my sister.

Some people have asked me over the span of my life how I feel about being adopted, and I always tell them the same thing. I'm extremely *grateful*, cause in my case my parents wanted children so badly that they highly valued my sister and me once they had us. I also tell them that, based on observing how a few of my non-adopted friends' parents treated them during our high school years, I would choose my fate over theirs every time. Blood-kinship does not necessary a parent make, I think, and at no time in my childhood did I feel anything but loved by my parents.

This is not to say they were perfect—and I don't know how one would even define what that means—but they were consistently nurturing and remained intent on making my sister and me feel loved. They were also strict, to some degree, and things like lying, laziness, and obstinacy were not tolerated. We occasionally were spanked, but that was rare and usually when we'd done something pretty far outside the established lines. (However, I currently think that corporeal punishment for children is wrong and counterproductive. There are negative aftereffects, and there are better ways to discipline a child).

I guess the thing I most take away from my parents is the model they established for my understanding of a romantic relationship and marriage. They truly loved each other, and every waking move they made was in support of each other. It was natural for them to kiss and say "I love you" at every parting occasion, and as I look back on it these many years later I consider their marriage to be the gold standard for how marriages and relationships ought to work.

As I said before, they provided a very loving environment for my sister and me. There were lots of hugs, "I love you's", and kisses from them both. In some ways, up until I reached the age of seven, you might say that our family was a fortress of love insulated from the rest of the world. They were such positive people, and this natural optimism rubbed off on me. I viewed life as a virtual wonderland, where good things were the order of each and every day. But, as is the case with all people, I suspect, the harsh realities of life eventually broke into our bubble of happiness, and it happened when I was seven years old. This was the sudden and unexpected death of my Uncle Lyman, which I described in an earlier chapter.

Shortly after my uncle's death we moved to Birmingham to start another business. My dad had left the entirety of the greeting card and novelty store he and my uncle had built to my aunt, which ensured that she and hers would be taken care of. It was a phenomenally profitable business in those days, before the big corporate competition came in and bought or drove out all their small business competition.

The Happiness Bubble Seriously Bursts

As I recounted before, I was seven years old at the time we moved to a fairly upscale neighborhood in the suburbs of Birmingham (Vestavia Hills). My dad was a hard (and smart) worker, and soon he had repeated the success he had enjoyed in New Orleans. Life was moving along quite nicely, and four years later we planned a summer trip to Kansas to visit my grandparents. It was to be a three-week trip, and we were all going to go. But my dad was in the process of opening a satellite branch of his business in Atlanta, Georgia, and he decided he needed to stay and focus on that project.

So one afternoon my mother, my sister, and I set out for Kansas. Before we left, we went downtown to hug my dad and say our goodbyes on our way out of the city. Our first destination was to be Enterprise, where my mother's mother lived, and then Lawrence, where my father's parents resided. So off we went, and a couple of days later we were at my grandmother Laeger's home. We spent about a week and a half there, and then left to travel due east to Lawrence.

What you must understand, in this context, is that I was not used to being that far away from my dad for long periods of time. We were extremely close, and he was as much a hero to me as to any boy who's ever been privileged to have a great father. I even hated it when my mom and he would go out for an evening of square dancing and would leave us with a babysitter. It was a rare occasion that they did so, but it always left me homesick for them.

About the time we left for Lawrence I began feeling excessively homesick for him, and after we had been at my grandparents' house for a week I underwent a horrible and hitherto-unknown experience. We were sitting at the picnic table in my grandparents' back yard eating supper, and suddenly an uncontrollable fear swept over me. I didn't know what was happening, and I looked at my mom and said, "I'm scared, Mom." She became alarmed, as did my grandparents, and asked me what was wrong. "I don't know," I replied, and I got up to walk around to see if that would help. But it didn't, and I was in unchartered waters about how to deal with this. I managed to calm down enough to get a little bit of sleep that night, but only a little.

The next day I wasn't feeling much better—I was still having a sense of overwhelming fear come over me at regular intervals—so my mother took me to the doctor. The doctor examined me and said he couldn't find anything physically wrong with me, and that maybe I was just homesick. He was 100% correct, and I later understood that what I was experiencing were panic attacks brought on by this extreme homesickness.

So my mother agreed to leave a day early to return home to Birmingham, hoping that reuniting with my dad would solve the problem. We left on a Saturday, and late Sunday afternoon we stopped in Cullman, Alabama to call my dad and tell him we were almost home (Cullman is only about an hour away from Birmingham). She called the house from a gas station, and one of our neighbors answered the phone. That was extremely odd, of course, and right away my mom knew something was wrong. The lady who answered the phone was JoAnne from directly across the street, a very good friend of the family. "Helen," she said, "Bill has had a heart attack and you need to come to the house as soon as you can." My mother said, "Well, I'll just meet you at the hospital there. Which one is he in?" JoAnne replied, "Well, come here first, and we'll go to the hospital together. You don't need to be driving any more than necessary." I think at that point my mother suspected that maybe he wasn't in the hospital at all, and that her worst fear had been realized. I credit my neighbor for not telling us the grim reality of what had happened, because she rightly feared my mother wouldn't be able to safely drive the fifty miles it took to get home.

On the way home, the three of us tried to offer encouraging words to each other, hoping against hope that he was still alive, and pledging we would do everything in our power to get him well. We finally drove into our driveway, jumped out of the car and started up the inclined sidewalk in the rear of our house. At about the same time our neighbor came through the back door and gave us the terrible news: "He's gone, Helen." All of us were struck dumb by her words, and we just stood there, crying and feeling a sense of shock.

I don't remember much else about that night or the following day, but on Tuesday my mother went to the funeral home to observe the body, and my sister and I stayed home. I remember hoping against hope that somehow, some way, he really hadn't died and that my mother would return with wonderful news. My state of denial was common, perhaps, but I think it was intensified by the general frame of mind that my storybook upbringing had instilled in me. You know, minor travails could occur in life—e.g., like when I once got a chicken bone stuck in my throat and had to go to the emergency room; or when I once stood in a bed of fire ants in a New Orleans cemetery and had severe bites all over my body; or when I once tried to climb up a water slide while another kid was coming down, resulting in my chin being split open on its jagged metal edge; or when I once got hit in the head by a bat at baseball practice and had to have numerous stiches in my ear—but nothing, and I mean *nothing*, came close to the utter emotional assault I experienced with the death of my dad. And it couldn't have happened in a worse way. I was physically sick from my homesickness for him after three weeks of being away, and then boom!—on the day we came home he had an early morning heart attack that killed him.

Of all the things in life that I have experienced and survived, I must say that that one fucked me up the most. After about a week of denial, the reality of life without him began to set in. My mother, God bless her, exhibited an incredible amount of bravery and selflessness through it all, and I suspect that her care of my sister and I helped to lessen the blow, however slightly.

But it's now fifty-six years since my father passed away, and I still miss him, yet I don't want to leave my discussion of him without mentioning some of the wonderful things he left me with.

Besides his teaching me how to pitch in baseball, he also taught me how to play golf. He would take me out in the front yard on Saturdays and Sundays and teach me how to grip a golf club and follow through with the swing. I was not as adept at golf as I was at baseball, so after a while we just stuck with baseball. He wouldn't let me play football, because he was afraid I would hurt my hands and be unable to play the piano, which I was beginning to excel in. Plus I was pretty scrawny compared to the boys who played in the grammar school football league, and I imagine he thought I might get seriously hurt. I rarely ever heard him cuss, and that only outside the house when he conversed with a neighbor who was a truck driver. He rarely ever drank alcohol, and that was only when we went out for seafood. He chain-smoked unfiltered Pall Mall cigarettes, and then Camels, and I suspect that contributed somewhat to his cardiac problems. But his family history was one of heart disease, and his dad (and probably his brother) eventually died of it. Once in a blue moon he'd tell an off-color joke when my sister and I were around, and I remember my mother rolling her eyes and simply barking "Bill!!!!" And by off-color, I don't mean risqué, but rather something referencing a bodily function or some other socially unacceptable thing.

My mother was a unique person, as well. After my dad died at age forty-seven, she took over his business and did the best she could to continue the life we had enjoyed up to that point. She was not as knowledgeable in business as he was, but she did the absolute best she could. We struggled financially most of the time she worked, and my sister and I were not able to wear the Jarman shoes, Gant shirts, and other symbols of upper middle-class status that most of the students in our high school wore. But we got by, and at a very early age I realized the shallowness of such social symbols. Nothing will teach you that quicker than being looked down upon by your peers because you weren't wearing the "right" kind of clothing.

She did the best she could with raising my sister and me, and as I got older I know I caused her much greater grief than her other child, mainly because I began to run with a crowd that did things she disapproved of. In high school, for example, I was all about going to the beer parties on the weekend, smoking cigarettes, cussing, driving fast cars and chasing even faster women. But in perspective, I wasn't rebellious, and my "sketchy" behavior wasn't out of control. And she and I were always as close as we were before I reached the age when I began to get a little wilder.

She was also unique in another way. There was not a hateful, deceptive, or manipulative bone in her body. She greeted every person she encountered with a friendly smile, and gave no weight whatsoever to a person's racial or economic status. I never knew her, even once, to lie or be deceptive—which is quite an anomaly in today's world. What you saw with her was what you got, and she was ready to hear your side of the story and believe you until you gave her reason to do otherwise.

I was privileged to have her in my life until I was fifty-seven years old, as she lived to be ninety-four. And I attribute my ease in relating to women due to her influence. I probably naturally get along better with the female population than with males because of it. When she died, it was of old age, and I saw it coming for a couple of years. This maybe made her passing a little easier for me than that of my dad, although it is much more recent and I miss her terribly.

My parents also introduced me to the second of the three major influences in my life—*religion*. They were not overly religious, but they were sincerely so. They were faithful members of the United Methodist Church, which was typical of the more liberal brand of Christianity that is ubiquitous in American culture today. We went to church faithfully every Sunday, and during the week we often participated in social events hosted there. Almost everybody in our neighborhood did, and the church functioned not only as a religious meeting place, but also a social one. My mom taught me to pray the "Now I lay me down to sleep" prayer at bedtime, and we always knelt by my bed and said it, at least until I was about ten or eleven years old. Like many other folk in America and across the globe, we regarded religion as basically consisting of going to church, living by The Ten Commandments, praying before meals and bedtime, and living an honest life.

I don't regard the death of my parents as one of the mines in my personal minefield, because losing one's parents is not unique to me. It happens to everyone who outlives their parents. Their passing certainly was an explosive force in my existence, but I had no control over navigating away from it. And as I said earlier, my nurtured and secure upbringing made exiting my personal minefield a little easier than it ordinarily might have been.

Chapter Five
HIGH SCHOOL DAYS

The influence of religion did not really take a serious hold on me until I was nineteen, but between my grammar school years and nineteen, I navigated through what used to be known as junior high and high school—grades seven through twelve.

I attended W.A. Berry High School in Birmingham, which housed all grades between seven and twelve. These days, what was known then as "Junior High" (grades 7-8) is often referred to as "middle school," and often is housed separately from high school. I can remember being somewhat terrified on the first day of seventh grade, as it was an unknown commodity, and I wasn't sure what to expect. But as time passed, I acclimated fairly well to the new environment, with one exception.

I think my dad's passing left me a little bit unsure of myself, and certainly very lonely, and I craved the acceptance of my peers. In those days at Berry, acceptance often came based on what kind of clothes you wore, what kind of home you lived in, and whether or not you could penetrate the various popular social cliques. Not much different than how the high school social scene breaks down today, I'm told, although I think it was slightly more pronounced at my school.

My dad's death also left our family in a precarious financial state, so I was not able to adorn myself in the aforementioned Jarman shoes, Gant shirts, and other accoutrements that guaranteed social acceptance. Still, I made do with what clothing we could afford, and I think my outgoing personality and musical talent helped me out a bit. I joined my first band at age thirteen, thanks to that $20 Sears *Silvertone* guitar I was able to acquire, and even though I was scrawny and middle-class poor I had the "cool" band thing going for me.

But it was not until the ninth grade that I was able to break through the barrier to social popularity and get what I thought was the acceptance I needed to make me happy. It came in the form of joining a fraternity. Yes, we had high school frats and sororities in those days, and if you weren't either a jock or a member of a frat or sorority, your social status was pretty much in the crapper. I joined one of the two "bad boy" fraternities available—Phi Delta Pi—thanks to the recommendation of a frat member with whom I had previously played baseball. And *voila!*—I was suddenly a member of the "In" crowd.

Yes, all of a sudden, the scrawny guy with no social cred was able to get all kinds of dates with girls who hitherto hadn't given him the time of day. And the "HI's" spoken to me in the hallways as students passed by suddenly quadrupled. Of course, as I look back on this state of affairs, I am appalled at how utterly ridiculous, shallow, and just plain mean it all was. Those who were prettier, richer, and whose families were more influential got Carte Blanche to the popular cliques. I just "lucked up" because I was a friend of a frat member who was looking to "rush" some of the local school freshmen he knew.

The Mines Get Bigger

Directly after my previously-described first fiasco with booze I mostly stayed away from it. It certainly didn't result in the fun and fancy I had expected. But my hook-up with this group of frat guys—a couple of whom remain friends to this day—started me on a path back to alcohol and into all kinds of other mischief. These guys were all about drinking beer on the weekends and trying to get laid. We cursed, smoked cigarettes, and were generally hunting the next great party. The frat was a real "Alpha male" kind of conglomerate, and even though that was not my personality, I tried to fit myself into it.

At the same time my musical interests had led me into another band—we called ourselves "The Trends" (how's that for a 60's name?!), and I was getting all kinds of love from everywhere. I had the frat, the band status, and even some of the "cooler" clothes necessary for my newfound social status. But after a couple of years of all this, I found that I wasn't really much happier than I was in the first couple of years in Junior High.

So somewhere around the beginning of my senior year, I pretty much ceased to participate in fraternity activities, and focused on my music. The Trends had disintegrated, and the kinds of music we listened to were increasingly those of the national counterculture associated with the Vietnam Era, so I kind of settled into the music and cultural atmosphere of "rebellion against the status quo." The true drug culture had not quite made it to our insulated upper-middle-class bubble, so I was not enticed by that until my summer out of high school.

Booze, Music, and Romance

Before I leave my reminiscences about high school, however, I'd like to touch on three experiences I had while a student at Berry. One has to do with booze, one with music, and one with religion.

The booze experience happened when I was fifteen, and it could well have been fatal. Talk about a dangerous land mine! I call the fiasco my "Drunken Cowboy on a Moped" experience. (A Moped, in those days, was essentially a bicycle with a lawnmower motor powering it; and I had pestered my mother mercilessly until she finally relented and let me buy it).

So my friend Jeff, whom I previously mentioned as the person who was "rushing" me into the fraternity, called one Friday afternoon and asked if I wanted to go with him and another guy to the local drive-in theatre for an evening of drinking and carousing. I, of course, said "yes," and told him I wanted to ride my new Moped to the outdoor facility. I imagine he thought that a little strange, but what he didn't know was that I had already been nipping at a bottle of bourbon I had stashed away somewhere. I was "cocked and loaded" (literally), and ready to party.

I then met Jeff (who was driving his car) and the other guy somewhere in the suburbs of Vestavia about a quarter mile from the theatre, and he told me to follow them there. He drove on ahead, and I fell in line and tried to keep up with his green Chevy as we wound through the suburban streets. He made a turn at one corner and began to extend the distance between us by a fair amount. So I kicked the Moped into "high gear" (which might've been 25-30 miles per hour) and made the turn, hootin' and hollerin' like a drunken cowboy riding his horse. I remember swinging one arm above my head, as if I had a cowboy hat in my hand.

What I *didn't* notice, however (by that time I was pretty buzzed), was a parked car just around the corner on the right side of the street. And by the time I saw it, I was moving so fast I had less than a second to think. And…..WHAAAAM!!!—I ran smack dab into the back of it. Somehow (and I still don't know how this happened), the force of the collision threw me off the Moped, over the trunk area of the car, and onto the soft grass of the car owner's yard. He was home at the time and heard the metal-on-metal impact noise, and came running out of his house. "Are you OK!!??, are you OK!!??," he screamed. I had evidently landed face down in the yard, and I noticed my nose smarting a little bit. But otherwise, I didn't have a scratch on me, and I told him I was "fine." It all happened so fast, plus I was more than a little buzzed at that moment, and I didn't really begin to assess the significance of the event until a little later when the police drove up.

But I answered all the officers' questions, and I'm not sure if they knew I was drinking or not (they probably did). At any rate, they loaded my Moped into the trunk of their cruiser and took me home. My mother just happened to *not* be at home that night (luckily), but I called over to her friend's house where she was visiting and told her all about it (minus the drinking part). She was alarmed, of course, but not too badly since I was home safe and apparently speaking quite rationally. (This event had sobered me up quite a bit).

As I looked back on that craziness, though, I realized it could have gone the other way. I could've hit the car, then been slung headfirst into the rear window, and I might not have been here to regale you with the craziness of my exploits through life's minefield. But fortune prevailed, and I'm still here to tell the tales.

The music experience came when I was a sophomore, just sixteen years old. The doorbell at my house rang one evening about dinner time, and a long-haired guy in bell-bottom slacks stood outside, accompanied by his mother. "We hear that you're a keyboard player," they said, "and our band needs one. You interested?" I thought it a bit odd that this guy, who appeared to be about my age, was escorted by his mother for such an errand. I learned, however, that the band to which they referred was named "Randy and the Rest," and that his extremely wealthy family was bankrolling it. As persons of some considerable means, they had quite a few connections in the recording business and the recording studios in Nashville. Randy, one of three sons in that clan, wrote music, and their plan was to make him—and by extension his band—famous. So we began rehearsing several times a week, and the family paid a professional photographer to come and take pictures of us. We recorded enough music for an album at a local music studio (Boutwell Recording), and the tapes were sent to Nashville to be mixed and mastered.

In pretty short order an album was pressed, and the family's influence enabled a single from it to be played on radio stations around the

Southeast. The first time I heard it on the radio couldn't have been more perfect. It was a Friday night, and I had just picked up my date Kim for the evening. As we left her house and travelled down the highway, our single came on. I let out a distinctive yelp, and my date looked at me with suspicion. "It's our song! It's our song!" I cried out; and, when she deduced that I wasn't completely whacko, she had the reaction I wanted her to have: "*I'm dating a rock star!*" Of course, I was *not* a rock star, 'cause the song only had regional airplay, and I wasn't even the featured singer in the band. But it was a thrill, nonetheless, and something I'll always have fond memories of.

The *real* memorable experience, however, happened shortly thereafter. Randy came to us and told us we were going to be the opening act for a "Shower of Stars" concert put on by one of the local radio stations in Birmingham (WSGN, 610). The line-up included The Vanilla Fudge, The Turtles, The Grass Roots, Bruce Chanel, and a few other acts which escape my memory at the moment. That was fun, but not long afterward we were told we would be doing another Shower of Stars show with even bigger stars. And I'd like to go into a little detail about that one.

The Beach Boys

The headliners for that show were The Beach Boys, and they were joined by The Strawberry Alarm Clock and The Buffalo Springfield. Again, we were the local opening act designed to kill time until "the big dogs" came on.

Perhaps the best way to relate this experience is to describe little snippets of events that occurred on the day of the show. The first happened in the afternoon, just after we had loaded our musical equipment into the auditorium through a rear loading dock. There was only one stage door in the rear, and it was manned by an older gent who looked like he had never heard a single note of rock music, or had ever seen a "hippie." Several of the artists were milling around the stage area, and suddenly we all heard some profanity-laced screaming going on near that back entrance. The screaming was coming from Dennis Wilson, the Beach Boys' drummer. Evidently, he had knocked on the stage door and told this door man he was one of The Beach Boys. It seems the man, who was employed locally by the auditorium administration, was not familiar with who The Beach Boys were. He had been rude to Dennis, and at first denied him entrance. This didn't go over too well with Mr. Wilson (as you can imagine), so he pushed his way in and started dropping "F" bombs at the top of his lungs, threatening that he would not play that night. A few of his band mates were successful in calming him down, however, and in a few minutes he was in a much better mood and began to throw around a Frisbee with his travelling companion—evidently one of those red-hot "California girls" memorialized in their songs. I remember thinking that these guys were genuine California surfer types, and their publicly peddled image matched their actual personas "to a T."

There was only one large dressing room in the whole auditorium, and I later happened to be in there at the same time one of the Strawberry Alarm Clock's members was. And in through the door came one of the Buffalo Springfield, and eyeing this Alarm Clock member, blurted out, "Oh, sorry, is this The Strawberry Arm Pit's dressing room?" The Alarm Clock musician quipped right back at him, "No, this room is reserved for The Buffalo Bullshit!!" And then both of them busted out laughing and gave each other a hug.

The next memory I have of that day came about an hour before the curtain was to open for the show. We were doing last-minute prep work before we went on, and Al Jardine of The Beach Boys walked out in our midst. He seemed quite friendly and humble (despite his status as a pop rock god), and he asked if there was anything he could do to help us get ready for the show. My thoughts were, "What a nice guy; he actually wants to help us nobodies do the best we can tonight." The guitar player told him he was having trouble tuning his guitar to my keyboard, and Al showed him a trick or two to make it easier.

The Buffalo Springfield

After we played our show (quite an exhilarating experience in itself), I remained backstage to ogle the massive collection of talent that was about to perform. Members of The Buffalo Springfield were standing in the wings, and I knew I wanted to at least say something to one of them. But I didn't have a clue as to what I might say. So I nervously approached one of them who was standing there with his guitar strapped on, and blurted out, "Uh, is that the guitar that you recorded *Rock & Roll Woman* with?" And then I thought, "Geez, what a complete buffoon you are to ask such a ridiculous question to a bona fide musical god!" But he smiled, and engaged me just the same. "No", he said, "that was a Martin D-28." Later on, I realized the person I was talking to was Richie Furay, who would go on to record some of the most iconic and sophisticated music ever to be heard around the world. The Springfield had just begun to be popular on the music scene, and at the time I didn't know the individual names of its members. But boy, would I like to have that moment back, because I was standing in the presence of Neil Young, Stephen Stills, Jim Messina, Richie Furay, and Dewey Martin. (I would have made a much bigger ass of myself if I had only known the historical significance of those around me). But they walked on stage, draped a huge American flag across one side of their wall of amps, and the crowd went ape shit. I can't recall their specific set list, but I know it included "For What It's Worth," "Rock and Roll Woman," and "Sit Down I Think I Love You." And there I was, just a naïve sixteen-year-old boy, standing ten feet away from them.

Good Vibrations

The final act, of course, was The Beach Boys. I remember standing there, still stage left, and being completely blown away by their vocals. They stacked five-part harmonies numerous times, seemingly with ease and certainly with precision. They were consummate musicians, writers, and performers, and they ended the show with "Good Vibrations." I remember thinking that it was hard to tell their live performance from that on their records. These guys were *the shit*, for sure. Great days, and great memories. But on to the other experience I mentioned, which had to do with religion.

A Short Tour for Jesus

A friend of mine at Berry, who had partied and pursued women with me over a couple of years, came under the influence of the national Campus Crusade for Christ organization. He caught the "Jesus fever" pretty seriously, and told me that I was a sinner and needed to get saved if I didn't want to spend an eternity in Hell. I was carrying around some general nagging feelings of guilt in my head, because my lifestyle was pretty much what was considered to be "sinful" by some in my immediate culture and certainly by my parents (e.g., the drinking, smoking, cursing, pursuit of sex, etc.), so I jumped on board for a few weeks. *But only for a few weeks.* My friend also eventually departed the faith, so to speak. But I think this experience sort of solidified how I felt about religious matters in general, and even though I did not continue with the lifestyle change and the related activities, I think I still thought that particular brand of Christianity was the true and right way. The answer to life's questions, if you will.

So high school was a mixed bag for me. I had sort of a love/hate relationship with it during those six years. I hated the shallowness of much of the social (classist) environment there—where rich, "well-born," and well-dressed got you acceptance and affirmation from your peers—but I loved the true friends, language education (I was a whiz in Spanish and English), and musical experiences that were also a part of it. And with this period of time I was thus well into life's minefield (music, religion, romance), but it would soon get more dangerous for me as the mines increased in size and intensity.

Chapter Six
THE SUMMER OF LOVE

About the time that I graduated high school, the drug and "hippie" culture hit Birmingham. Many of my friends began to experiment with the elements of that counterculture, which of course was mostly about "sex, drugs, and rock'n'roll." The drugs, in our geographical corner of the world, mostly included pot, hash, mescaline, and acid. Cocaine was not readily available or even familiar to most folks, and heroin was almost non-existent locally. (This was long before the wholesale prescribing of opioids for pain, as is now common).

The generally accepted lifestyle centered on drugs, rejection of all social and economic status norms of the day, and of course free and unfettered sex. I began to grow my hair out that summer, I suspect because it was more of a new sort of social status than a symbol of rebellion. I also experimented with drugs. Although beer and wine were still my "go-to" party libations, smoking pot and hash were my first forays into pop pharmaceuticals. I liked the sensation of hash—in fact, I liked it very much—but not so much the pot. Pot made me feel overly focused on my own thoughts, and kind of gave me a weird head sensation. I mean, I could hear things going on behind me that I never noticed before, and I didn't much like it. But the hash, for some reason or another, was different. I really liked it.

Hallucinogenic drugs were also readily available at the time, and my first "trip" was on mescaline. I was introduced to it by a bona fide "hippie" from Atlanta named Tad, and we "dropped" the substance about 8:00 PM one evening, which resulted in us staying up all night and playing our guitars. He was also the person who introduced me to "finger-picking" on the instrument, a technique using the thumb, index, and middle fingers. I still sometimes play the guitar that way to this day. But I liked the sensation of mescaline. It was mind-altering, but not in a scary way for me.

Off to "Hot-Lanta"

My next experience with psychedelics came during a spontaneous trip to Atlanta, Georgia. Two of my friends and I decided one afternoon that we would travel there to purchase some hallucinogens, because we had heard that it was readily available at various places on Peachtree Street in the heart of the city. My cousin Ken, who was a committed Mormon and the only sane one of us at the time, heard us talking about the trip and asked if he could go along. And I knew what he was thinking. Although he definitely didn't approve of what we were about to do, in his mind he was saying, "These guys are going to get all drugged up in a town three hours away and they'll have no way to get back." And he was dead right. I don't know if I ever thanked him for his very kind concern for our well-being, but I'm going to make sure that happens before either of us exits the planet.

So off we went in my 1965 convertible Ford Mustang on a Sunday night. We got to Atlanta about midnight, Georgia time, and found our way to Peachtree Street. We hopped out of the car and began randomly walking down the sidewalk, and pretty soon we spied two guys leaning against a storefront. We approached them, like morons, and asked if they knew where we might "score" some drugs. Luckily, they told us they were in possession of some and asked what kind we wanted. "Oh, you know," we said, "pot, hash, mescaline, acid—stuff like that." They ducked off somewhere down the street and in just a few minutes returned with the goods. And I will never forget the names of these two pharmaceutical street salesmen: "Trip" and "Lucky." I swear, you can't make this stuff up. They were two serious "freaks" who were living the counterculture dream.

If it seems odd to you that such things were readily available on the open street in major cities during those years, consider the times. Law enforcement wasn't nearly as concerned as they are in present times with drugs and street prostitution. I visited New York City in 1981 and the same was true. There were cops on every corner, and in between them—up and down almost every block—were pimps, street hookers, drug dealers, and card game scammers. They would lean against the storefronts, and if you looked at all like a potential customer they would step out and ask you if you might be interested in whatever particular commodity they were selling. I suspect the cops just considered this to be mostly non-violent activity that was not worth their time to confront.

But back to the Atlanta trip. We left Atlanta at about four in the morning, having ingested some acid and having smoked some pot. It was early September and the weather was still warm, so we dropped the convertible top. My cousin, of course, was driving this band of lunatics back home, and was occasionally laughing at our increasingly inane conversation as we "came on" to the acid. I suspect, in his totally sober state, he became amused after he had heard "far out!" and "oh, wow!" for the umpteenth time.

At any rate, we pulled into Birmingham and headed towards Vestavia where we all lived. We exited the main road and pulled up to a four-way stop which was immediately adjacent to the local grammar school—and the three of us who were tripping *freaked out*. Here we were, in a convertible Mustang with the top down, totally exposed at an intersection where all kinds of cops, mothers, fathers, and little children were congregated at 7:30 AM on the first day of school. Our acid-induced state of mind made us paranoid to begin with, and the presence of cops, little children, and parents made us all certain that *everybody there knew exactly what we were doing, and that we were going to go to jail immediately!* Of course, nothing was further from the truth, as my sober cousin was driving the car perfectly well and wasn't doing a single thing to draw attention to us. But we nonetheless begged him to get us out of there and to the house where we would feel safe.

That event was typical of a handful of other similar occurrences over the ensuing months, and at some point I had a moment of clarity. It seemed to me that drinking or smoking pot was one thing, but hallucinogens were quite another, and that they were very likely doing some serious damage to my brain. So I never did them again.

Life Questions and An Approaching Big Mine

This particular summer was also significant to me because I had begun to become dissatisfied with my life in general, and was pondering the purpose of it all. I mention my state of mind here, as it was critical in setting me up for a seminal confrontation with a big land mine in my life: my sincere conversion to evangelical Christianity in May of 1971.

Between that summer and the next May (of 1971), I attended my first semester of college. I had enrolled at the University of South Alabama, a fairly new college in Mobile. I remember standing in the class registration lines one sunny morning that September, with no clue whatsoever about what I wanted to do with my life. I felt totally helpless and overwhelmed. I mean, here I suddenly was at *college,* being asked to choose a life-long profession. I hadn't really thought too seriously about the subject, mainly because I was too busy partying and playing music throughout high school. I ended up choosing Business Administration as a major, but I did so mainly because I didn't know anything else to choose. Business, at the time, didn't really interest me, but neither did anything else. I felt totally lost.

After a semester there, I transferred back to the University of Alabama in Birmingham, where at least I could be at home in familiar surroundings. I studied (or more accurately, attended class) for two semesters there, leading into the spring.

During this time I felt somewhat confused, particularly about the seeming frailty of life. I thought to myself, "What is the purpose of all this? Why am I spending what would probably amount to four years of my life studying things that don't interest me, particularly in light of the fact that the Soviets could launch a nuclear attack on the U.S. at any time, which would almost certainly mean the end of all mankind?" I felt like a leaf detached from a tree, blown about randomly in the wind.

I did, however, engage my musical interests a bit during these days, and I want to relate a couple of those experiences, mostly due to their humorous nature.

Beginning My Musical Career

At some point I hooked up with a couple of musicians from across town, possibly at a "hippie" club ("The Nexus"?) I would occasionally frequent in downtown Birmingham. (Or possibly through a mutual acquaintance we had who was from Vestavia Hills. I don't rightly remember). These two guys had been playing in a band by the name of "Clinton." I don't know the reason for the name choice, since the political Clintons were not even on the national radar at that time. But their guitar player had quit, and they were looking for someone to replace him. I was heavily into the guitar at that time, and I agreed to meet and jam with them. They were good—*real* good—and their tightness made it evident that Vernon (the bass player) and Don (the drummer) had been playing together for a considerable period of time. They were real "freaks"—Verne had waist-length hair, Don wore tie-dyed clothing and said "far out" a lot—and both of them always had some good "bud" to share. We immediately gelled musically, and set out to book some gigs.

Our first gig was at a beer joint in downtown Birmingham named "The Starlight Club," and it was quite something. There were two dance cages on either side of the stage, and there was always at least one "go-go" dancer in them every time we played. One night, I took a particular fancy to the dancer on my immediate right. She was tanned, with olive skin, dark flowing hair (sound familiar?), and was built like a brick shithouse. She was dressed in a skimpy red-sequined costume and quite adept at "go-go dancing" (whatever that actually is), and I offered to buy her a drink after work. She accepted, and about a half hour later I found myself inquiring whether she'd like some company for the night. She was about ten years my senior (probably around 30), and she just smiled and said, "Thanks, but I'm going home by myself tonight." In her eyes I could see that what she really meant was, "Thanks, sonny boy, but you're obviously without any real-life experience, you're too scrawny, probably broke, and I'm too old to play the one-night stand game." I still smile when I think about it.

But an even more humorous experience happened when we booked our band to play a party for the Association for the Blind in Birmingham. It took place in a small commercial loft downtown, and there were about a hundred folks there, most of whom were in fact blind. Now, since we were a three-piece band with only guitar, bass, and drums, we compensated by using large amps that produced quite a bit of volume. What I'm trying to say is, we were *loud*.

After we had played our first couple of songs, one of the gentlemen in attendance approached the stage with a note written on a napkin. In my mind I was thinking, "Oh good! Someone already has a request for a song, so they must really like us!" I took the napkin from him and read the following words: "Just so you know: We're blind, not DEAF!!!" I was a bit taken aback, but I chuckled under my breath, and immediately told Vernon and Don we needed to turn the volume down.

And thus began my career in what would later morph into a high-powered land mine: Playing music on the club circuit. What would happen in the next few weeks, however, would change the direction of my life forever.

Chapter Seven
SAVED!

When I returned home to Birmingham in 1971, I began attending class at UAB—the University of Alabama at Birmingham. My days consisted of going to school, and my nights were filled with either tooling around and partying with friends or the occasional band practice. I felt very directionless when it came to what I wanted to do with my life, and my two quarters of study at UAB didn't provide any hints for me in that area. I remember flunking Psychology 101, doing only slightly better in Biology 101, and being totally disinterested in all things academic. I did, however, manage to take a couple Spanish classes which I aced, but that was only because foreign languages were something I had always loved.

I was sort of drifting through life, rudderless, wondering what to do with myself. I had no girlfriend, no meaningful employment, and I just sort of "was." And then it happened.

I don't exactly remember where I ran into them, but two very attractive and "freakish" girls invited me to what they called "a new kind of church" that met in a local high school cafeteria on Sunday nights. "Hmmm," I thought, "I'm not too intrigued by the notion of religion, but I AM intrigued by these two girls who seem to have an interest in me!" So off I went a day or two later to hopefully meet up with these two and see what this "new church" thing was all about.

When I arrived there, about a hundred people were sitting around, waiting for the service to start. A lot of them were my age or slightly older, and the dress was extremely casual—jeans, tank tops, tie-dyed shirts, and the like. They seemed excited about something, and many of them were overtly friendly towards me.

And then the pastor came out, also dressed more casually than most pastors I remembered from my earlier days. It was clear from the get-go that he was a high-motivation type, and he didn't miss a beat over the next hour—he led some singing, praying, testimonials, and Bible reading with great verve. I had heard the message before and as I mentioned before had experienced some light interaction with "religion" on occasion in my later teens. But at the end of the festivities that night, this preacher gave an "altar call," and for some reason I felt I needed to respond to it. I was one of about twenty people who did "come forward," and of course there were all kinds of "spiritual high-fives" going around from those in attendance after it was all over.

It was then I spied my two "temptress" friends who had invited me to the gathering, and they told me to come sit in their van with them for a little while. We all piled in the back of the thing, and they fired off the big question: "Did you DO it?," by which they meant "Did you accept Christ as your Savior?" I said "yes"—and probably would've said yes even if I *hadn't* (they were girls, for crying out loud!)—and I was suddenly smothered with all kinds of hugs from them, accompanied by their jubilant screeching. I thought to myself, "This is what I've been looking for," but was probably not quite clear whether it was the female attention or the religious conversion that was the major source of my joy.

I'm not quite sure how deeply rooted my "conversion" was, but it was at least minimally sincere, and as the summer progressed I became more and more committed to what I thought was the ultimate truth in life. There were Bible studies, church activities, baptisms at somebody's lake house, and all kinds of intense socializing going on all the time. At the very least, I was getting lots of needed human interaction, and I was finally pretty happy and content. I was noticeably at peace with myself, and (I thought) with God, and nothing else really mattered.

The Next Step – Bible College

Somewhere near the end of that summer, the older brother of one of my high school friends came by my house one day and invited me to sit down for a chat. He had been converted also, and was sort of the "older spiritual brother" to many of my acquaintances. His name was Bob, and he was an outgoing and athletic type. His older brother Mike was, at the time, a famous linebacker with The Miami Dolphins, and Bob's whole clan were well-known and respected in the community. We sat on the couch in my living room, and he put a pretty serious question to me: "What do you think about going to Bible College in September?" I already had one year of college under my belt, and I was not particularly enamored with either of the colleges I had attended. So I thought, "Why not?" That "why not" started me on a path that would mould a great deal of my subsequent life.

When I put this idea to my mother, she was not as revved up about the possibility as I was. "Jim," she asked, "what kind of employment can you expect with a degree in *Bible*?" (A wise woman, indeed). But she was, in general, quite happy about my conversion experience—I imagine because I had stopped hanging out until all hours of the night with questionable company and coming home half drunk. So she agreed to pay the first semester tuition at the local Bible college in our city. And from there on my life would never be the same. I had stepped on a land mine with my conversion to evangelical Christianity, but I was about to ramp up the lethality of that explosive device with the depth of religious indoctrination I received at that school.

The name of the institution I gained late entrance to was Southeastern Bible College. It was a fundamentalist and socially hyper-conservative institution. There were rules about long hair on men (it wasn't allowed), slacks and ties were required for attending class, and no jeans were tolerated. We had to "look the part," whatever the Hell that meant. After all, they were training preachers, missionaries, and Bible scholars.

For women, dresses were required for class attendance, and they could not be shorter than one inch above the knee. Low neck lines, or otherwise tight clothing, were not permitted. The penalty for breaking any of these rules began with being "campused," which meant not being allowed to leave your dorm room other than to attend class. Too many violations would earn you a ticket to expulsion.

Doctrinally, they were fundamentalist, or "evangelical." They were also Protestant in terms of theology, and particularly a dispensational, pre-millennial theology that taught that "The Rapture" would be happening soon, possibly "any day now." For them, the Bible was the eternal and error-less Word of God, and any science or philosophy/theology that contradicted it was regarded as a pack of lies from Satan.

I was not too terribly happy with the social strictness that was imposed there, but it was not such a big deal to me since I now considered myself *saved*, and thought such minor matters were, well, minor matters.

I was a bright person, I suppose, but I had never been a highly disciplined one when it came to school. Heck, I barely got out of high school with a "D" average, and that was only because my American history teacher let me take my senior final exam a second time, and all but told me beforehand what the questions were going to be. I guess he figured that I, and my other two friends who were in the same boat, would end up in worse shape than we already were in if we didn't at least get out of high school with a diploma. Or perhaps it was that he would rather pass us than see our faces back there in the coming year.

However, there was one general subject that I had loved in high school, and I aced every class I took in it. That subject was language—whether foreign or English. I loved the mechanics of it, and things like diagramming sentences in English or learning Spanish really cranked my tractor. (I know, I'm a freak!) I took three years of Spanish, aced them all, and was even the President of the Spanish club in my senior year. It's a good thing I liked something, because I would never have gotten that passable "D" average if I hadn't!

So when I got to Bible college, I took a course in Greek as soon as I was allowed to do so (I believe it was in my second year there). And pretty much from that moment on I was academically focused like never before. I aced most of classes I took, and added Hebrew language to the mix. The Bible, of course, was written in Greek (the New Testament) and Hebrew (the Old Testament, though small parts of it were written in the related Aramaic language).

My obsession with Greek and Hebrew was encouraged by my professors, and a couple of them even met for extra translational studies with me, and with my friend Chris, who was also obsessed.

I eventually ended up in their newly established graduate school, which provided even more coursework in the two languages. After I graduated in May with their Master's degree in Biblical Studies, I even taught two semesters of introductory Greek in the undergraduate school that summer.

I could go on about lots of other, not-so-pleasant things that happened during my four years there—like a couple of my friends getting expelled for having "a bad attitude," a beloved professor getting booted from the faculty for screwing one of his students, another friend who hung himself in his dorm room, the sudden and unexpected death of a couple students and professors I knew well, my attempt in my first year there to sneak a young girl into my dorm room for sex (I was temporarily "backslid," as we called it), and my disgust with a couple of the "counselors" who were seemingly there for the sole purpose of handing out demerits and confining students to their dorm rooms on the weekends. But overall, my experience there was a positive one, and I believed that I was right where God wanted me to be.

The Beginning of Doubt

During most of my time at Southeastern I was standing squarely on what later turned out to be a land mine (although I didn't know it at the time), but the seeds of my eventual departure from Christianity were planted one evening (in my junior year, I think) as I sat studying one of the Gospels in my dorm room. (Yes, my departure was ultimately caused by an intense study of the Bible itself!). I was reading the passage in Matthew about Peter's denial of Jesus at the time of His arrest by the Roman authorities. In that passage, Jesus says, "Before the cock crows, you will deny me three times" (v. 26:34). As I read and pondered it, it occurred to me that I had read about the same event in another Gospel, and that it said something quite different. So I cross checked it, and sure enough, Jesus said "Before the cock crows twice, you will deny me three times" (Mark 14:30). I thought to myself, "Hmmmm…..these two accounts of the same event seem to contradict each other." But since I was heavily indoctrinated into the notion that every word in Scripture was written by God, and therefore could have no factual or historical error in it, I filed it under the "I don't get it, but I'm not going to worry about it" category. This was the sort of cognitive dissonance that I think many conservative Christians have today. If something doesn't seem quite right in the Bible, they just blow it off, because such questioning is regarded as sinful, or evil. Or perhaps they just don't *want* to think about such matters, because it would disturb the faith which they have appropriated to meet their deep emotional needs.

As time passed, however, and I continued my personal Bible study and went on to graduate school at the University of Wisconsin, I became aware of hundreds (if not thousands) of contradictions within the pages of the Bible, as well as massive contradictions between what we know from science and what the Bible teaches about the origins of man and the universe. But, for the next several years after this discovery in my dorm room, I still regarded the Bible as "Holy Writ" in a very real sense.

It was also during my time at Bible College that I met and married my wife, who was an equally committed Christian. She was quite pretty, and more "hip" than most students on campus, and our common relational foundation was the spiritual one. We dated for about three years, and during the summer of 1975, a year before I went to graduate school in Wisconsin, we married in a beautiful little chapel in Birmingham that exhibited stained glass windows and European stone architecture. That chapel still stands today, and is as gorgeous as it ever was.

I can't leave this account of my Bible college years without mentioning a professor of mine that exercised an enormous influence on me. His name was C. Gary Staats, and he had earned a doctorate in Old Testament at Dallas Theological Seminary, a conservative Texas institution that provided about half of the faculty at Southeastern. He was the quintessential nerdish intellectual prof, and his obsession was the Hebrew language. He would teach his classes, then come find me and my friend Chris and get us to sit down and read the Old Testament in Hebrew with him. He loved doing this, as did we, and we would spend hours talking about translational issues and the meaning of the Scripture. His excessive adoration of Hebrew rubbed off on me, and he encouraged me to write to the Hebrew Department at the University of Wisconsin main campus in Madison to inquire about graduate studies there. I was more than interested, and after my time at Bible College I enrolled by mail in extension classes there. I took about four classes—all devoted to reading, translating, and analyzing linguistic issues in certain books of the Hebrew Old Testament. This was, to me, like I imagine heroin is to a heroin addict. I was pumped up about it, and I applied for admission and was accepted.

So, in the summer of 1976, my wife and I were off to the quaint city of Madison, Wisconsin, and to a new and somewhat different culture than either of us had hitherto experienced.

Chapter Eight
OFF TO GRAD SCHOOL

My recovery from stepping on the land mine of religion took a major step forward with my education at the University of Wisconsin-Madison. It was the first time I had a chance to really study "the Scriptures" in an environment where there was no religious bias or theological presupposition. There were no teachers trying to tell me the "underlying meaning" or "theological significance" of any book or segment of the Bible. There were just highly educated, empirically-oriented men and women who let these documents speak for themselves, as we translated them from their original languages and in the historical and cultural context of ancient times. The move to Madison, however, involved a geographical move to a culture that was quite different from the one I grew up in.

Culture Shock

For a person who grew up in the culturally conservative and sunny South, the state of Wisconsin is a brutal lesson in culture shock. The people there speak with quite a different "accent" from that of American Southerners, and my wife and I stood out like sore thumbs. I remember the first day we arrived there and popped into a McDonald's to grab some lunch. We were standing there in line (or "on" line, as they would say), and as soon as we began speaking nearly every eye in the place turned on us. I'm pretty sure they thought, "Who the Hell are these hillbillies?," because both of our accents were pretty Southern at the time. We laughed about it later, but this was my first introduction to Midwestern culture.

The other brutal reality of that state is the weather. Here in Alabama, the worst elements of winter are occasional sub-freezing temperatures and, once in a while, a snowfall or two. We were NOT prepared for that onslaught of God-awful sub-zero temperatures, continuous snow from about November to April, and the occasional blizzard. For a Southerner, this was a miserable agony that never seemed to end. My God, in January the temps never got above zero—even in the daytime—and the snow piled up week after week, which wreaked great havoc on my toesies when I had to walk in it. I remember countless times when my feet and fingers went numb, and I was sure they would've broken off if I had banged them against something solid.

But we managed to find a small apartment there, and both of us found jobs in the summer before I started school in the fall. My wife worked at a Gimbels Department store, and I found a job as a clerk at a gas station/Quik-Stop. I later found work painting apartments, then as an hourly wage worker in the Hebrew Department and, ultimately, as a teaching assistant in the department after I had completed my Masters degree.

The UW Campus

From the first day I set foot in Van Hise Hall, an eighteen-story behemoth of a building where language and cultural studies are housed, I was psyched. I LOVED the Hebrew department, the professors, the massive campus that is home to forty thousand students, the beautiful historic architecture that comprises most of the buildings there, the libraries, the old book stores and jazz bars that adorn the adjoining State Street, and the culture in general. The sheer volume of cultural activities going on in that town is mind-boggling, and it immediately fed one of the big three elements that have dominated my life—my inquisitiveness. If I'm not learning something at least once a day, I start to experience withdrawal symptoms. (The "lack of information DTs," if you will). Of course, you can learn all kinds of things *anywhere* by observation, reading, watching TV, thinking, and speaking with others. But this town, and the cutting-edge university that it hosts, is a veritable Mecca for an information sponge like me. If there is a "Heaven"—and I have no idea whether there is or not—I hope it's a lot like Madison. This homeboy loves him some of that town. I was fortunate to be able to revisit the city about three years ago, after being gone for more than thirty years, and very little has changed in and around the campus. The same buildings are there, sporting about the same appearance, and State Street (which leads to the Capitol building) is still very much a beehive of activity. Of course, some things have changed farther out and away from campus, which I discovered when I couldn't even find the farmhouse that we occupied about twenty miles outside of Madison in my final year there. I suspect that it was torn down.

When I finally began classes that first Fall, I knew this was what I wanted to do with my life. I LOVED language. I LOVED studying the Old Testament. I LOVED being introduced to the manifold other languages that were necessary to do scholarly work in Hebrew—Phoenician, Punic, Syriac, Ugaritic, Aramaic, proto-Semitic, and etc. I LOVED studying about the archaeology of the Middle East, and the numerous visiting lecturers from Israel and various domestic academic institutions—Harvard, Yale, and The University of Chicago's Oriental Institute. And I LOVED studying the classical Greek that I minored in for my doctoral program. Get the picture? If it had to do with learning about biblical things, or ancient culture in general, I LOVED it. I still do, although the amount of time I have for such study is considerably less than it was in those days as a full-time student.

Evolving Out of Christianity

And it was during my study at the UW that I began to seriously evolve out of the fundamentalist dogma that I had so sincerely embraced since I was 19. The reason for this evolution is pretty simple. I studied the Bible in its original languages, without any theological discussion of its "meaning," and in an open and honest academic environment where the independent literary meaning of each individual book was the only concern of my professors. Not ONCE did any of them advocate a religious belief or suggest that the Bible was anything more than the surviving literature of the ancient Hebrews. For example, one semester I took a course on the Book of Job, and our task as grad students was to translate it, defend our translations using comparative language and literary sources, and advance our idea about what the author (and/or editors) of this book was trying to say. There were no voices in that class, or any other, which told you what religious significance must be attached to it, or how it fit into some grand theological scheme cooked up by Middle Age theologians, or anything of the sort. Each book was treated as an independent literary composition. And language, comparative literature, archaeology, and ancient translations and commentaries were adduced to try and figure it out. But getting to the overall message was especially tough for a book like Job, primarily because you get all kinds of disparate ideas being expressed within it, and the existing structure itself suggests we may not have all of what was originally penned by its author or redactor(s).

Yes, I was like a kid in a candy store. Even though the UW was academically tough, the weather was awful more than half the time, and we were poor as church mice, I was doing something that I genuinely loved. This environment was Geek Central, and I was in Geek Heaven.

But the die was cast. If you have an open mind, and come to the Bible with no presuppositions, you cannot come away with the conclusion that it is anything more than the philosophical and theological musings of a long list of various Hebrew authors and institutions. It simply is not rational to believe that it was "inspired" by any god, and hence that Judaism or Christianity is an expression of anything supernatural. They are, like all other theological or philosophical systems, merely the attempts of man to explain what can often be a bewildering and mysterious existence. The world, and our experiences in it, are sometimes overwhelming, and it is to be expected that human beings in all ages would attempt to discover some certainty regarding its meaning and purpose. I think the idea of meaning in life can be answered individually, and there will be vast differences in how people see it, but clinging to a religion or system that claims divine authority is simply not one of the legitimate ways to do it.

However, even after all of my time and studies at the University, I wanted to believe that there was some kind of supernatural reality to my Christian faith, even if the central Book on which it was ostensibly based was not the absolute "Word of God." I guess I looked at the Bible as an imperfect record of a perfect Jesus and God, and that my faith still had validity.

A Bonus Gift—A Little Girl!!

It was during my time at Wisconsin, however, that the first of the two best things that ever happened to me in life occurred: My wife and I had a baby girl.

I remember every detail of that blessed process, from our discovery of the pregnancy to the day we carried our little girl home. I was thrilled about it, as was my wife. But in those days, the ultrasound technology that shows a fetus's gender was not yet widely used in the United States. We knew we were going to be parents, but we didn't know whether our baby was a boy or girl. So we decided to reserve a name for both contingencies.

We agreed on a name for a girl pretty early on—Alexandra Brooke. But we couldn't quite decide on a boy's name, and to say that we waited until the last minute is a gross understatement. My wife began to have contractions late one night when we were living in that farm house twenty miles from the hospital, and we were timing them. We figured we better make a decision pretty quick, 'cause it was midnight and the contractions were at "go time" intervals. So we threw up our hands, and said "OK. It's going to be Matthew Reed." Ten minutes later we were in the car and headed to the hospital.

It was December, and therefore "colder than camel hump," but thank heavens our car heater was working well. We arrived at the hospital, were met with a wheelchair by the hospital staff, and were whisked away to a private room. It was a good thing, too, 'cause Brooke decided to make her appearance just three hours later a little after 5:00 AM. I was, of course, new to this kind of thing, but I was allowed into the delivery room and watched as she poked her little head out into the world. It was something I'll never forget, although the whole thing seemed almost surreal.

By about 7:00 AM my wife was back in her room, we had made the necessary calls to our families in Birmingham, and I headed down to the nursery to again see my little bundle of joy. I remember standing at the observation glass, and thinking, "Holy shit! I'm not just someone's child anymore, I'm now a *parent!*" It was a sea change in my self-identification, and it hit me pretty hard. In a good way, of course, but nonetheless in a life-changing way.

A little later in the day they let me hold her in the hospital room, and I was just blown away by how tiny her fingers, toes, arms, and head were. For the first time I experienced what billions of my fellow earth travelers had previously experienced, which was the profound nature of a father's love for his child. I would experience it one more time in my life, but that happened about ten years later, and I'll get to it in my narrative.

So a day after her birth there we were, standing at the entrance door to the hospital, ready to take our new bundle of love to our home in the countryside. The problem was, as I mentioned before, that it was about five degrees above zero outside, and I was a little freaked out about exposing Brooke's fragile little frame to such hostile weather. But having no choice, I wrapped her blanket over her and covered her whole body, and began that brutal walk from front hospital door to car door. It was only about a thirty-foot walk, but I was afraid the chill would have an adverse effect on her. It did not, and we made it back home and laid her in a sea of blankets in the warm baby crib we had waiting in our bedroom.

The Decision to Return Southward

After I had graduated the Masters program, taken a year of doctoral classes, passed the Ph.D. preliminary exams, and begun my dissertation, I decided to leave my Mecca and return to Birmingham.

The actual decision to leave Madison, however, came at a specific moment on a specific day, and I remember it like it was yesterday. It was an overcast afternoon in January, and the glum-looking skies matched the glum forecast: extremely cold temps, snow, with high winds moving in. We needed groceries, however, and I told my wife that I'd pop into town really quickly and pick them up. We lived exactly eighteen miles outside of the city of Madison, having lucked up in finding an old two-story farmhouse situated on four hundred open acres that were slated for a state park development. The state wanted somebody to live on the property while they ramped up to do the land renovations, probably to scare the youngsters away from partying on the property and tossing beer cans and other debris everywhere. They only wanted $125 a month rent for it, and my wife and I jumped at the opportunity.

So off I went into Madison to pick up the groceries, thinking that I could get it done and be back in about an hour, before the bad weather moved in. I should've known better, because it began to snow before I even got into the city. After about thirty minutes of shopping, I came back out into the open air and realized I had screwed up. It was snowing like a bat out of Hell, the wind was blowing pretty hard, and the temperature had dropped to somewhere around 15 degrees below zero. The roads back to our farmhouse were fine, because folks in the Midwest are extremely efficient at keeping them ploughed, but I knew there would be the matter of navigating up our driveway when I returned. The driveway stretched about 1/8 of a mile long, and the state ploughs did not service private property.

So I got back to the junction of our driveway and the county road, and there were at least four inches of new snow on it. It was the only path to the house, and I knew I was in trouble. So I pulled off the main road, maybe two feet into our driveway, and grabbed the two sacks of groceries. The wind was blowing at about 35 miles per hour, the wind chill factor was about 40 degrees below zero, and the total overall accumulated snow depth had to have been at least 8 inches. In short, I couldn't *see* shit, I couldn't *feel* shit, and I knew I was in *deep* shit.

And then a moment of clarity, an epiphany if you will, descended on me and punched me right in the face. It happened this way: I started the trek up the driveway back to the house, each arm laden with a twenty-pound sack of groceries. I couldn't walk at a normal pace, cause my feet sank deep into the icy, wet snow with each step. It was so bloody cold that it made my nose start to run. And then it happened. BEFORE THE LIQUID CASCADING FROM MY NOSE COULD HIT MY UPPER LIP, IT FROZE! Yes, it just froze in transit right there on my face, like someone had hung icicles from my nostrils; and a voice reverberated through my head: "YOU HAVE TO GET THE HELL OUT OF THIS PLACE!!!" I remember this event like it was yesterday, and I hoped that this was my first and *final* experience with a bona fide blizzard.

I did, however, finally make it back to the house after about thirty minutes, with absolutely no feeling in my feet and hands, and with a face that I imagine resembled Jack Nicholson's at the end of *The Shining*. There was extreme exhaustion present in every inch of my body, but at least we had groceries.

This was January of 1979, and as soon as summer hit and I was out of school, my wife and I hightailed it back to Alabama. The ninety-degree temperatures, dry landscape, and rolling green countryside were like oxygen to a drowning man, and I swore I'd never return to the brutality of a Midwest winter again. My oath, however, was to be short-lived.

Chapter Nine
A SHORT STINT IN MICHIGAN

After returning home to the bright, sunny, warm, and thoroughly comfortable climate in Alabama, I spent a little over a year looking for substantial enough work to support my wife, our new bundle of happiness (Brooke), and myself. I looked everywhere I could think of, but nobody in town was beating down anyone's door looking for a Hebrew teacher. Finding employment in our corner of the South with a degree in ancient Semitic languages was like trying to find a needle in a haystack, a virgin in a brothel, or a shadow in the dark. It wasn't going to happen. So I reverted to working whatever jobs I could find, which were mostly related to painting apartment complexes and houses. I was disappointed, of course, that I had spent a lot of time, effort, and money obtaining four collegiate degrees, only to be forced to do something totally unrelated to any of my education and experience. But hey, it was honest work, and the few dollars it produced kept us afloat.

Needing desperately to find well-paying employment—particularly since I was the bread winner for three—I responded to an ad in a trade publication for a person with Old Testament academic credentials and at least a working knowledge of Hebrew and other Bible-related subjects. It had been placed by the managing editor of a new project that William B. Eerdmans Publishing Co. had taken on. They were revising and updating the very popular *International Standard Bible Encyclopedia*, and they needed an additional copy editor.

I contacted Eerdmans, they interviewed me, and *voila!*—they hired me. Of course, the job was *in Michigan,* and I knew it required me to break my "never again in the North" oath that I swore during the blizzard/grocery shopping fiasco in Wisconsin. But *t*his job offer was a huge gift in my estimation, because it was one of only a few jobs nationwide that required my particular set of skills and education. Yes, it meant returning to that miserable, damnable climate, but the opportunity was just too good to pass up.

So in January of 1980, I packed up all of our possessions into a U-Haul, and set out northwards. As it turned out, Grand Rapids was not quite as brutal a clime as Madison was, probably because of its position just east of the Great Lakes, which mitigated the cold winter blasts coming eastwardly into the U.S. down the Arctic Corridor. I must clarify that it was not *as* bad, but it was still pretty darned cold in that city.

At any rate, I settled into my new job as copy editor, and fell in love with both it and the staff at Eerdmans. Our particular project involved four main people: Ed, the project supervisor, who had a Ph.D in New Testament from Claremont University in California; Gary, a Calvin College graduate with extensive biblical studies background; Robert, who was finishing his Ph.D in New Testament studies from a British University that escapes my memory at the moment; and myself.

You might think at first glance that this cadre of intellectuals might be a stuffy lot, but I can assure you, the exact opposite was true. They were smart, but they were anything but stuffy, and they also knew how to party. We worked hard all week, but when the weekend came, the beer flowed and we frequented the bars. We had a great working relationship all around, and coordinated our efforts in between trading jokes in the break room and discussing all kinds of unusual topics. I must say that the rest of the staff at Eerdmans was equally friendly, and we were all sort of a big family that socialized outside of work.

As far as my academic interests were concerned, I was in "hog heaven" in that city. It was home to a number of colleges and universities, as well as Baker Book House, Zondervan's Publishing Co., and Kregel Publishing Co. Along with Eerdmans, these publishers had bookstores where you could pick up "seconds" for little or nothing. (Seconds were, of course, books that often had only a blank page or two or some exterior blemish, but were otherwise perfect.) On my lunch break at least once a week, you could find me in any of these places, spending a dollar or two to build my library.

It was during this two-year period at Eerdmans that I further evolved out of my religious fundamentalism. I had lots of "face time" with the Bible itself, editing tons of articles submitted by very respectable scholars worldwide who, while still being members of the conservative Christian faith community, were mostly not fundamentalist in their scholarship and viewpoint.

So my stepping off of the land mine of religion was in progress, but I was not fully there yet. I sort of had "one foot on, one foot off" of it. And I'd like to point out that some of my most anxious times were during this period of *limbo* in my beliefs. Prior to that time, when I fully believed that I had escaped Hell and was on the way to eternal bliss, I rarely had much angst about the subject. And of course when I finally realized that Christianity was not true, I had virtually no such anxiety. But this "in-between" period produced a lot of fearful introspection and anxiety in me. You have to remember, when I was converted, I was not a "fair-weather" Christian. I believed in it hook, line, and sinker. And I believed that Hell was a very real place where everybody except true "born again" believers like me were going to spend eternity.

It was also during this time that my wife and I were reaching a point of impasse in our marriage. We had been having problems for quite some time; and, after being in Michigan for about six months, we separated and were eventually divorced. My wife moved back to Birmingham to be close to her parents, and my daughter went with her. This was a tough time for me, particularly since I was separated from my daughter, whom I worshipped (and still do). And in fact, a little over a year later I could stand being away from her no longer, so I left the Eerdmans project to return to Birmingham so I could be close to her.

I'll never forget the overwhelming joy I felt when I drove into Birmingham, knowing that I would be able to spend time with my little girl, at least on the weekends. The first weekend I had her, I took her outside for a walk around the condo complex parking circle where I was staying at the time, and I just wept the whole time. She may have thought that I was crying because I was sad, but these were truly tears of joy.

However, I was again faced with an old problem—how to find employment in a city and state that had no use for my particular skills and education.

Chapter Ten
HEADFIRST INTO THE LOUNGE CIRCUIT

Safely back in familiar surroundings in Birmingham in the summer of 1981, I was optimistic about life in general. I would be able to see my little girl on regular occasions, and I had some income guaranteed from a long-distance editing project I had been given by Eerdmans. The weather was fantastic—warm, to be specific—and things were looking up.

My widowed mother and her new husband had agreed to let me stay with them for a while until I could find full-time work and get a place of my own. So I set out to apply to every local academic institution, book and magazine publisher, and Jewish community center around. I submitted resumes to Birmingham-Southern College, a private United Methodist school of some repute, but they require at least one degree from a Methodist seminary if you teach in their religion department. I also applied to Samford University, another private college with Baptist ties, but the answer was the same: I had no Baptist credentials. I applied to a fledgling seminary being set up by the local evangelical Presbyterians, but the problem was that I no longer believed in the nonsense of biblical inerrancy, or even the divine inspiration of the Bible. In my conversation with the pastor who was directing the seminary's creation, I told him I was only interested in teaching Hebrew or Greek, and that I would not express my views on any religious topics. He just sat there, half smiling and looking at me sideways, but I knew what he was thinking: Not just "no," but "Hell, no!" I fully understood his attitude.

I did manage to get some part-time teaching work with the University of Alabama in Birmingham in their adult continuing studies program, but it was only one "Survey of the Bible As Literature" class that paid just slightly more than the cost of the gas it took me to get to the class building. I loved it, however, and I think my 12-15 students did also.

My next set of interviews was with various local magazines in and around the city. *Southern Living*, a popular and widely distributed magazine focusing on horticulture, food, and all things having to do with…well…Southern living, agreed to interview me. "What do you know about flowers, plants, southern cooking, and such?," was the first thing they asked me. I responded, "Uh, well, I, uh………," and I knew I needed to politely dismiss myself. I also applied to a book publisher in Montgomery (Alabama's capital, which is about ninety miles south of Birmingham), thinking my editing skills might put me in good stead with them. But again, no go.

I began to get desperate, because my Eerdmans money was about to dry up, and I had already stayed too long at my mother's residence. She wasn't complaining; but, Holy Moly, I was 29 years old and living with Mom!

At some point after several months of job hunting, I came to a realization. If I was going to stay in Birmingham, I was going to have to find employment in something totally unrelated to my graduate studies. I was denominationally too unaffiliated to teach at the Methodist or Baptist colleges, I was too religiously liberal to teach at any fundamentalist institution or church, and the Jewish folks noticed that I wasn't a descendant of Abraham. Everyone with whom I had interviewed was very friendly, but they just were unable to offer me work.

[Parenthetical fact: I have since learned, from the DNA-based ancestry site "23 and Me," that I am 49% Jewish!! I have Ashkenazi-type Jewish blood running through my veins, and that *may* have helped me when seeking employment from the local synagogues and Jewish centers, but I doubt it. My life, up to that time, had not been culturally Jewish.]

Hawking Radials

So I began to seek employment in the newspaper want ads, job fairs, and just about anywhere I could. I did a few manual labor things with a temp agency, but the $2.30 an hour wasn't going to cut it. Then, one evening, I saw an ad on the television. It was from one of the local job fair outfits, and it said that *National Tire Wholesale*—a business that sold and installed car tires (if that wasn't obvious)—was hiring several inside sales people. I called, got an interview, and right off the bat was offered a full-time job. I guess they were impressed with the two Masters degrees on my resume, 'cause I sure as Hell didn't know the first thing about tires. They gave me a book about tire basics to study, which I did, and the next Monday I reported for work.

The job entailed standing behind a counter, operating a computer, and basically selling tires to people who came in off the street. It was pretty easy, although standing up for eight hours a day was pretty tiring. I was young, however, and I made the best of it. I liked my co-workers, most of whom were a fairly wild crowd of early twenty-somethings who were always partying when they weren't working. We sold tires, smoked cigarettes, breathed tire dust, and told raunchy jokes all day long for six days every week.

I remember thinking, "Just a couple years ago I was translating Ugaritic language symbols into English, reading Syriac inscriptions, and for what? To sell tires?" It's not that I thought I was above selling tires, but that I could've gotten that job without knowing the first letter of the Hebrew or Phoenician alphabet. But it was work, it paid well; and, after six months, I was made assistant manager of that store.

Musical Land Mine Ahead

About six months in, however, I was glancing through the "Help Wanted" ads again in the paper, and saw something that caught my eye: "Keyboard player wanted for full time bar gig!" "Oh my God," I thought, "here's something I can do, and it would be fun!" I also figured I could work my full-time day job and do this at night, and have all kinds of money floating around!

So I called the number, and the band leader said "Come on down and sit in for a song or two so we can see if you're a fit for us." So, after work, I went down to the Ramada Inn in the southside of Birmingham, boarded the elevator for the sky lounge on level seven, and sat down in the back of the room. The band was playing Top 40 tunes, and they sounded pretty decent. They had a cute female vocalist who could really wail. So during the band break I tracked down the guy who seemed to be the band leader, and told him I was the guy who had called about auditioning for the job. He said, "OK, we'll call you up during the next set and you can play a few songs with us." He did, and I played, and it went very well. So he told me he'd call me the next day after he'd had time to talk to the other members of the band. He called, as promised, but not with the news I wanted. The female vocalist in the band had a boyfriend who also wanted the job, and he was a pretty good musician, too, so they were going to give him the job. I was crushed, because I really wanted that gig—not just for the money, but also for the opportunity to meet….you guessed it….girls. Girls seemed to like guys in bands—regardless of whether a band was good or bad—and this band was pretty good.

But we don't always get what we want (nod to the Rolling Stones), and I continued on with my tire job. Then, one day just two weeks later, I got a call from that same band leader. "You still want a job?," he asked, and I said "Hell, yes!" It seems the keyboard player and his girlfriend had broken up, and she told the band leader she wasn't going to stay if her ex continued in the band. And since she was a bigger asset to the group than he was, he got the boot. And thus began what was to be a long stretch of being a full time musician on the club circuit in the metro area of Birmingham—a twenty-year stretch, to be exact. Little did I know that I had stepped on a major land mine that would nearly kill me in subsequent years.

So for the next several months I played the lounge gig from 8 PM to 1 AM, then was back at work selling tires at 7 AM. When I even *think* about that schedule now, I get tired. But I was just thirty years old, and my immunity to "tired" was much higher than it currently is.

However, the grueling schedule was too much for even the young me after about six months, and I was faced with a decision: Play six nights week and make about $400, or do the 50-hour-a-week day gig and make about the same. So I chose the music route, and it was to take me to places and introduce me to experiences the day job never would have.

I could write an entire *War-and-Peace*-sized history on the things I experienced during those two decades, but I won't, for a couple of reasons. First, I don't want to embarrass my children with some of the more outrageous circus behaviors I engaged in; and second, I don't want to alarm my readers with some of the more dangerous aspects of it. So a few examples will suffice to demonstrate the level of crazy that I was subjected to (and willingly participated in).

I'll start by relating what I myself first noticed about suddenly being a professional musician. On the last Sunday before I set foot on stage the next evening on Monday, I had caught the interest of only a few girls every now and again. After I stepped up 6" onto that low-slung stage that Monday night, female interest in me immediately reached an epic level. I could float a tasteless joke about how 6" makes a big difference here, but I won't.

Yes, the ladies suddenly saw something in me that they hadn't seen before, and I was loving it. I no longer had to go out and about to try and meet them, 'cause they came to where I was, and in large numbers. I would soon learn that this new-found interest in me was a pretty shallow one for most of them, 'cause the small number that I actually considered having a relationship with would look at me funny when I told them I wasn't going to be in the band business forever. And sometimes they would lose interest when they found a guy in a better band or at a more popular club.

But in the early days I didn't care, 'cause, after years of loneliness, I was having fun with the large numbers of women chasing me and, of course, with the frequent sex. And every night was a party of sorts, complete with lots of beer, shots, and even occasionally a fat blunt. It was an ethereal world, a surreal and never-ending ride of inanity, signifying next to nothing.

I realize that plenty of people have met and married (or cohabited with) their significant other in bars, and I don't mean to diminish the importance of them as a hunting ground for meaningful relationships. But the type of bars I played in were of course loud party venues, with excessive drinking (and drugging), and it was a rare occasion that any conversations I had with the opposite sex penetrated any significant subjects.

Chapter Eleven
TWENTY YEARS AS A KEYBOARD WARRIOR

Once I had quit my day job and devoted myself to being a professional musician full time, I found myself with more energy to stay out later *after* our gigs. This meant either frequenting after-hours clubs that catered to musicians and bar service people, or hanging out in the home of some young lady whom I had met in the club. As I mentioned before, the sheer number of stories I could tell is massive (twenty years' worth), but I'll mention only a few of the highlights (or more accurately, *lowlights*) from about 1984 to 1994.

<u>Hands In the Air!!</u>

The first that comes to mind is what I call the "hands in the air" event. It happened at an after-hours club named "Hogan's," which was *the* place to go for musicians and bar service personnel after work. It was located in the basement of a four-story office building situated in downtown Birmingham. It had a fire occupation level of about 300 people and, except for Monday through Wednesday nights, there were about that many people congregated there. It opened at 2:00 PM in the afternoon, and closed every "night" at about 7:00 AM.

I was playing there in the early 8 PM to 1 AM slot with a band called "Wolf Creek," and we were followed by the house band that played from

1 AM to 5 AM. At some point during the three or four years I played that club, I had "dated" one of the waitresses, whose name was "Mary." And by "date" her I mean that I had engaged in erotic activities with her a couple of times. I was not aware of it at the time, but she was a possessive sort; and, for her, the sex meant that I was in some sense her exclusive beau.

So one Sunday night, when I was off from playing, I went into Hogans and sat with a couple of off- duty waitresses at a table in the back. One of them, named "Tish," was a good friend of mine with whom I had worked in another club. The other waitress, "Kara," I think, was a good friend of hers and incredibly sexy. I had seen Kara before, and was insanely hot for her, so this Sunday night was beginning just right for me.

It just so happened, however, that Mary was on duty that night, and *we were sitting in her section*. (You see where this is going). So here she comes, tray in hand, and with a look that was none too friendly. She probably knew me well enough to discern what my intent was with my two table friends, and I don't think she much liked it. I would eventually find out how much she didn't like it, but one thing at a time.

Tish, Kara, and I sat there that evening for about two hours, listening to the band and throwing back shots every fifteen minutes or so. The talk then turned to what was on the agenda next, and Tish suggested that we all pile into her car and head to her house. I was delighted, knowing what the likely outcome would be. So I paid our tab, and we got up and walked out the front door of the club, which was adjacent to the upper level gravel parking lot used by Hogans' clubgoers. Little did I know that a very jealous and angry pair of eyes had followed us to the front door, and that soon the feet associated with those eyes would follow suit.

My two lady friends and I had made our way out the front door and to Tish's car, which was parked about midway down the graveled lot. Parked next to her car was a cargo van, which blocked our vision to the path that we had just trod getting there. We stood there next to her car for maybe a minute, just talking and laughing, and out of the corner of my eye I thought I saw someone or something coming from around the side of that cargo van. Before I could turn, I felt the stinging pain of a hand across my face, and I turned to see who or what had delivered it. Whoever it was said nothing, but merely delivered the blow and disappeared around the end of the cargo van. I *knew* who it was, however, and I immediately walked out to the end of the van to ask her (Mary) what the Hell was going on. I called to her as she headed back towards the front door of the club, but she wouldn't turn around. About that time I heard my friend Trish scream out "You fuckin' bitch!" at Mary, and then I heard and saw something I'll never forget. From the corner of my eye I saw the low-lying cloud cover above us light up brightly white, and simultaneously I heard what sounded like a full-fledged cannon go off behind me. It jarred me, and I wheeled around to see Tish standing there next to her car, smoke pouring out of the barrel of a .357 Magnum pistol she held in her hand. I said, "What the fuck, Tish?," a little dumbfounded at what had just happened. She said "I'll shoot that little bitch for that. She can't fuck with my friends!" Aware that things had gotten *way* out of control, I approached Tish, not sure of what she had in mind next. I figured I had just better try to talk her into a calmer state, lest things escalate into something we all couldn't return from. After calming her down for a couple minutes, I figured I better go back in the club for a minute and try and calm Mary down also, so I made the turn around the side of the van and headed towards the front door. My head was sort of down as I came around the van, as I was thinking about what to say to Mary, when I heard these words pierce the air: "Freeze, and put your hands on your head!!!!" I looked up, and there—in a staggered semi-circle—were nine cops frozen in place, all with their guns drawn down on me. There were Birmingham cops, county cops, and a couple University of Alabama-Birmingham cops all waiting for me to make an offensive move. Of course, I obeyed the cop's directive immediately and froze, placing my hands slowly on top of my head. The head cop approached me and screamed in my face, "Did you just discharge a firearm, Sir?" I said, "No Sir," but he wasn't buying it. He continued to scream directly in my face, not so subtly suggesting I was lying, but just then one of the other cops moved out in the circle wide enough to notice Tish and Kara standing between her car and the van. He directed his weapon at them, and asked them the same question my cop had asked me. Of course, Tish, being the ballsy chick that she is, responded "Yes, I did. That little whore assaulted my friend over there, and I don't put up with that shit!"

After a few minutes, the cops had figured out what had happened and that nobody had actually been shot, and they began to interrogate us all about the event. In the meantime, Hogan himself had exited the club to see what all the flashing bubble gum machines in his parking lot were about. He, of course, knew most of the officers on the scene, and eventually talked them out of pressing any charges against anyone. In fact, all that they did to Tish was empty the ammo out of her gun into her back seat, put the gun in her glovebox, and tell her to get her ass home. They told me to do the same, and I was more than happy to oblige. But, dammit, my plans of a ménage a trois with my hot friends had been foiled, and I'm sure Mary got the last laugh about it all.

The next day, I found out how the cops had gotten there so quickly after Tish fired the shot. It seems one of them, a Birmingham officer, was driving down the street immediately adjacent to the club at the precise moment she squeezed the trigger. Of course, he KNEW what that sound and light show was about and hit his radio immediately for back up as he turned into the parking lot. And since the UAB cops were patrolling that general area all the time, it took them no time at all to answer the call.

As I think about how close I came to becoming a statistic that night, I can only smile and imagine that I must have been "livin' right." Living right??? — probably not—but at least living *lucky*.

Sex on the Couch

Another event during my tenure as a Birmingham lounge musician bears telling here, I think, since it further illustrates how crazy things were in those days. It happened in a ritzy Holiday Inn that contained a beautiful lounge on one end dubbed "The Moonraker." This lounge had tiered, amphitheater-type seating, plush carpeting, chandeliers hanging from the ceiling, mirrored glass on the interior support posts, and a little upstairs terrace where a couch and a cozy fireplace were situated. It was a classy joint, to be sure. The band I was playing in was a show band, and we dressed in varicolored, bright tuxedos every night for our performance.

On one particular Friday night the club was wall-to-wall with partygoers, and the registers were clanging with record liquor sales. Some of those sales were to the band, and by midnight most of us were in a fine mood. So we took a break, and I began to mingle and chit-chat with the patrons. At one point, I remembered I needed to ask our bass player about something, so I looked around this sea of boisterous clubbers to try and locate him. I couldn't find him in the main room, so I figured he might be on the upper terrace with the couch and fireplace. As I ascended the walkway to the terrace, I saw the back of his head as he was seated at one end of the couch, which faced the outside wall of the room. I tapped him on the shoulder from behind the couch, and he turned his head so he could see what I wanted. Over his shoulder I noticed the long hair of a female whose head was positioned in his lap, and I assumed she was just lying there for a minute during our break. However, as I started to round the end of the couch, I noticed that her head was not stationary, but was rather bobbing up and down. Yes, she was "servicing" him orally, and she seemed not to notice anything else in her surrounding environment. Now, this might not have struck me as too unusual, 'cause most musicians I knew in those days were sluts and whores of the worst kind—myself included. We screwed in hallways, at the top of club staircases, in bathrooms, in parking lots (in and out of vehicles), in club offices, and generally anywhere where it was not raining. But we usually did it in a private way, which is what made this particular event so amusing. I mean, we were knee-deep in people who were standing around in that room shoulder to shoulder, and the only partially open space was that couch. I glanced at my bass player buddy, he gave me a devious grin, and I exited the terrace trying to control my laughter. I can only assume that the people standing around in that room were completely snockered, or otherwise just too engaged to notice the *felatio* going on right beneath their noses. At any rate, we laughed and joked about it for months afterwards, and I vowed to myself that I was going to "one up" him with some slightly more outrageous debauchery. But the opportunity never presented itself.

These were the *modus operandi* of most musicians I knew in those days, and I was no different. But even through the haze of the alcohol-fueled nights and the endless revolving door of party girls, I had always wanted something more. I was looking for my significant other, my love, someone with whom I could lose my heart, share life, and have a stable and committed relationship. During my twenty-year run on the club circuit I came close to finding it a couple of times, but the relationships always ended up being more superficial than I initially thought they might become.

<u>A Blessed Interlude</u>

In the middle of all this craziness, however, something *did* happen in 1989 which I regard as the second of the two greatest events of my life: The birth of my son in August. His mother Lisa and I had known each other for six or seven years prior to that event, and we had gotten together from time to time. One of those times happened to leave her with child, and nine months later I found myself in the delivery room early one weekday morning. As I mentioned earlier, I had already seen what a live birth looked like when my daughter was born, so I figured I was a veteran at the experience. And when the doctor signaled that the baby was beginning his final exit and that I should come and observe, I pranced right over, feeling confident. But for some reason, this time was different. As Dalton popped his head out and took his first look at the world, I suddenly became faint and got a little wobbly in the knees. The doctor looked up and said, "Maybe you better go sit down," and I think he was a little concerned that he had *three* patients in the room instead of two. But I regained my stability and soldiered on. To this day I have no idea whatsoever why I lost it during the delivery of my second child, but maybe it was because I had not eaten anything that morning.

At any rate, my health was of no relative concern at the time, because Dalton's birth was fraught with serious problems. He came out fine, but his normal transition to outside oxygen did not go smoothly. I carried him from the delivery room immediately to the ICU, cause the doctors were extremely worried about his condition. His oxygen saturation was only about 15%, or about a sixth of what it should have been. When they had completed extensive testing a few hours later, they gave his mother and me some bad news: They figured he only had about a 20% chance of surviving. This sent his poor mother into hysterics, and was a serious punch in the gut to me.

He survived the night, and for the next two days the hospital staff tried everything they knew how to do to get his oxygen levels to come up. But the levels didn't move, and we all were just numb from it.

Somewhere around the third or fourth day, however, they approached us with an idea. They had been in contact with an elite neonatal facility in Kentucky, which had offered to fly down and pick Dalton up so they could try some procedures that were available there. We, of course, were happy to try anything, because the local prognosis was bleak.

So a doctor and two nurses flew into Birmingham and came to the hospital and got him. They hooked him up to a number of machines they had on board the plane, and off they flew towards Kentucky. And then the most fantastic and unexpected thing happened. When they had achieved their maximum altitude after take-off, the machines began to register some totally odd and unexpected numbers. His oxygenation system had kicked in, and he was suddenly getting all the air he needed. The numbers, suddenly and unexpectedly, were *normal*. He was breathing totally on his own, and was looking like a normal baby without the blueish tint.

They got him to Kentucky and did a large battery of tests just to make sure all was well, and it was. They called us immediately and told us the good news. We, of course, asked what they thought had occurred during that flight. They said that they weren't sure, but that it was possible the change in cabin pressure at peak altitude may have caused his respiratory system to fully kick in. They said they had seen such a thing happen before, but only a time or two. Of course, we didn't care *how* it happened, just that it *had* happened. So that was the beginning of my son's sojourn on this planet, and today he is a healthy, highly intelligent, and well-adjusted 30-year-old working in a tech job out East. He recently met and married an all-around lovely person named Kate, so his tenuous beginnings have given way to a fortuitous life. I am most happy when my children are happy, so these days I'm pretty happy.

So I look back on that general time period now with some sense of fondness, even if I was half-broke and hungover most of the time.

"You Can Be A Star"

Some other things happened during this general time period, things which also made my journey a pleasant one. One of these came in 1990 when I was playing in a pretty good Top 40 house band at another Ramada Inn near the Birmingham airport. It was a four-piece band, and our forte was both Top 40 Pop and 60's and 70's R&B. We were pretty serious about our musicianship, and we rehearsed a lot. One day the drummer/band leader came to us and asked if we would like to compete on the national TNN (The Nashville Network) channel in a "You Can Be A Star" contest format they were running. Our first response was, "Hey, we're not a country music band," but he assured us that the producers wanted bands that played any genre of music, and that we stood the chance to win a big cash prize and a recording contract. So of course we were in, and we rehearsed about three songs incessantly before the day came to head to Nashville.

When we arrived, we were housed in the Opryland Hotel in two plush rooms, and were escorted about by some local PR people. The next morning we were required to show up at 7:00 AM in the main TV studio, so the show's producers could talk to us all about what to expect during the taping of the show. We got there and joined about a dozen other performers and musical groups in a bleacher-type seating area. The head producer told us that three of us would tape for each show, and actually all of us would tape on that one day for TV distribution over Monday through Friday. The four final daily show winners would tape the final winner's contest show that was to be shown on a Friday. We all nodded and indicated that we understood.

The next thing he did was designed to calm those of us who had never been on TV before. I had been on a few times (local TV), but many there had never been in front of a camera. So he started out by teaching us a simple phrase that he wanted us to repeat. That phrase was: "It doesn't mean shit!!!!" Yes, he made us repeat that phrase over and over about 10 times in unison, usually interspersed with his commentary. He would say something like, "I'm not going to be nervous today, because ….." and then point at us to shout in unison "it doesn't mean shit!!" Or, "I'm going to be relaxed when the camera lights come on because...". You get the picture. (And he was one hundred per cent correct. In the long run, it didn't mean shit, even for the winners).

So we all went to our dressing rooms and got ready for the taping. When we came out on stage, I was overwhelmed by the amount of technical hardware that was associated with this theatre. Besides the massive sound room off to one side, there were cameras positioned *below* the stage, *even with* the stage, *above* the stage, and even one that flew *over* the stage, attached to a wire stretched above our heads. Since we were taping, there was no live TV audience out there and I didn't experience much nervousness at all. We came out, were announced by the hosts (who, incidentally, were Sawyer Brown's guitar player Bobby Randal and TNN personality Lisa Foster), and away we went. We had rehearsed our first song so many times that performing it was second nature. We finished, the audience of other contestants and studio personnel clapped, and we exited the stage to watch our competition. And, lo and behold, at the end of that segment we were declared the winners by the judges, and they told us we needed to stick around to tape the next day's show.

So about an hour later, there we were again, wailing away and feeling good about our chances. But fate was not to visit us as kindly in the second round—we lost to a three-man acoustic group which played pure country music. But we were fine with the outcome, 'cause we were going to be on national TV twice in the coming weeks.

So, after scavenging around the massive lobby of The Opryland Hotel and staying overnight in these plush accommodations, we were on the road back to Birmingham and our little lounge gig. But it was fun, it was enlightening, and I think we all were glad we had agreed to do it.

Just for kicks, I decided I was going to watch the airing of the two shows in a local bar, so I could enjoy surprising the bartender and the patrons with a "Turn on the TV, you're gonna see somebody you know!" moment. Yeah, I know; I was being an attention whore. But it was all a lot of fun, and I regret none of it.

During the rest of the early 90s I continued to play full time as a musician, and I worked a couple of day jobs here and there as well. But somewhere in the middle of that decade it occurred to me that I had better begin plans to transition out of the lounge gig business and into something that might have a more stable future attached to it. The house band business was quickly shrinking, due to a number of factors: People weren't going out as often due to stricter new DUI laws, and the tech revolution had provided for entertainment at home more than ever before, the result of which was that club owners had fewer profits with which to pay bands. When I first began playing the circuit, there were more full-time club jobs available than there were good bands to fill them. By the mid-90's, however, the opposite was true. Many club owners shifted to having bands only on the weekends, or substituting the much-less-expensive Karaoke format for live musicians.

So I began searching for day work again. Among the several jobs I performed were cell phone sales, credit card terminal sales, and home improvement sales. The home improvement job, which involved selling sunrooms for Sears, was to have an enormous effect on what I ended up doing through the 90s and up to the present day.

At this point—the mid-90s—I guess you could say I had squarely stepped on the pretty powerful land mine of being a full-time lounge musician, *and I survived it.*

Chapter Twelve
GETTING A "REAL JOB"

So here I was, in the middle 1990s, in my early forties, and in a profession that was slowly but steadily offering fewer opportunities for musicians. I should mention here that I engaged in a brief marriage (about a year and a half in duration) in 1995 with a Canadian citizen I met in a hotel lounge gig. We got married for all kinds of wrong reasons which I won't mention here, except to say that "being madly in love" was not one of them. My daughter Brooke adored her, and she herself needed a legal basis upon which to remain in the country, so I thought, "Why not?" I should've sat down and thought about that question more seriously than I did, but it's alright because the divorce was amicable and only took about a half hour to process. But during that brief time I got serious about searching for a stable (and less dangerous) line of work. I worked for a BellSouth cellular phone agent for a couple of years, then saw a Sears ad for a home improvement salesman. I applied and got the job, and ended up working for them for the next three years.

The Sears job was my entry into a sector of business that keeps me employed to the present day, but the journey from that initial job and what I do today was a rocky one. When I first responded to the Sears ad about sunroom sales, I knew nothing about construction, home improvement in general, or any such thing. Heck, I was a trained musician, and an academic who could translate languages and interpret ancient literature. In fact, I had little or no interest in learning about two-by-fours, the insulation ratings of windows, or concrete slabs. The first time I discovered I had to "stake out" a plot in someone's back yard for the construction of a sunroom, I felt a sense of despair. It made me feel like everything I had pursued and become interested in during the first four decades of my life was for naught. I was depressed.

Another issue associated with taking a job in home improvement sales was the fact that I am not inherently a "high octane" salesperson at heart. I'm no Billy Mays or "Sham-Wow" guy!! My philosophy about selling things was, and is, to present the product and price to a prospective customer in a pressure-free way, then let that potential customer call me back if they are interested. But this was the exact opposite of what Sears was training us to do. In a five-day initial training session in Nashville, the trainers spent four and a half days teaching us how to apply pressure to the homeowner to sign a contract *right then and there*, and only a half day on the sunroom components themselves. They referred to this process as the "one-call close." I remember thinking, "What the Hell have I gotten myself into here? I don't want to do this."

But my options were few, if any, at the time. I *had* to take a more stable direction for the future, and so I decided to stick it out. So I came back home from Nashville and started the sales routine. At first, I was not very successful, 'cause I was almost apologetic about the fact that I was asking a person to make a decision *in our first meeting* about a product which ranged in price from $6,000 to $40,000. Most people were put off by the "this price is only good for today" routine, and I was in full sympathy with them. So I began to stray from the high pressure approach demanded by the company and—to make a long story short—when I left the company three years later, I was the top Sears home improvement salesperson *in the country* in my final month.

This experience made me realize two things: Home improvement in general can be sort of an artistic endeavor, and I could be an effective salesperson. The reason I left Sears at that time, however, was because I got tired of selling $100,000 worth of products each month for them and only getting paid about $4,000 for my effort. I thought, "I'll bet the pay is better in some local home improvement companies around Birmingham, and I have the experience now to do well in that niche."

So for the next couple of years after I left Sears I worked for two different home improvers in central Alabama, and I did pretty well. But I ran into another problem with them that I couldn't live with. The owners of these companies were men with very little conscience and an abundance of greed, and they were constantly goading me to raise the prices I was asking for the things I was selling—vinyl replacement windows, vinyl siding, sunrooms, etc. Unlike the procedure with Sears, where all prices were fixed, we had latitude in determining the asking price. And I was always setting prices at what I considered to be a *fair* level. My bosses in these companies would haggle with me, asking me why I didn't "stick it to 'em." I would tell them that building a business in the long term could best be done by doing quality work for a fair price, 'cause eventually these same people would discover that we had "stuck it to 'em" and would tell lots of other folks about it. (You know, because bad news travels a lot faster than good news does). But they were not having it, I suppose because they were so blinded by greed that common sense was not an available resource to them. The worst case of ripping people off I witnessed in either of these two outfits came when one of their other salesmen came in one day bragging about how he had sold an eave siding job to an elderly black lady for about $14,000—a job that was going to cost the company less than $1500 total to install! I thought to myself, "How do these assholes sleep at night?" And so around that time I made a decision that would affect the rest of my life.

I thought, "You know, I'm a reasonably intelligent person, I understand the home improvement business pretty well now, I have contacts with installation crews, and I bet I could build a business based on quality and fair pricing if I just tried." It was a hard decision I was faced with, 'cause I would be cutting ties with a few established contractors in the area, and I only had about $300 of spare change in my pocket with which to start a business. But after pondering it for a couple of weeks, I decided to make the leap.

I told my then-current boss that I was leaving, and he told me I was crazy. And, as I recall, other people basically told me the same thing. But I was determined, and I set out to try my hand at entrepreneurship.

With no money for advertising of any kind, I was stuck with composing flyers and doing a sort of "knocking on doors" thing. After I obtained a business license with the state, I began calling folks I knew to see if they knew of anyone needing what I was offering. The response was tepid, at best; and I began to think I might have made a colossal mistake. But one day I got a call from someone who knew someone I knew, asking if SEAL-TITE (the name of my new company) installed vinyl siding. I was so thrilled about it that I arrived 15 minutes ahead of the appointment time and put on the most positive demeanor I have ever displayed. After measuring the house and calculating the price, I told them that $4800 would get their entire home covered in maintenance-free vinyl. They said "yes," I nearly jumped out of my chair with glee, and I was off to the races for the next twenty years doing various kinds of home improvements for a living.

Of course, it has not all been rainbows and roses, 'cause running your own business has its pros *and* cons. In my first year, for example, I had a customer write me a bad check for $11,000, after I had spent about $9,000 in materials and labor totally revamping the outside of his home. And $9,000 was not a hit that my business could easily absorb, 'cause I was small potatoes, running on a very small budget. Thankfully, when I turned the bounced check over to the worthless check division of the local District Attorney's office, this person somehow found the funds to pay me fairly quickly. I guess the "make this check good or we'll be back to transport you to the county hotel" ultimatum the D.A. gave him got his attention.

And, of course, developing deep enough pockets to be able to start spending money on a very complex set of advertising options took a while. You can spend a boatload of money on bad or ineffective advertising, and there is no end to advertisers who constantly call you, claiming that spending your dollars with them will make you rich. But after twenty-plus years of building the business, I have finally found a reasonably efficient way of making a good profit while maintaining integrity of operation.

During the first ten years I was in business, however, I was forced to continue to play music part time—mostly on weekends—cause both income streams were necessary to survive in any comfortable way. But I'll never forget the first time I realized I no longer had to spend my weekends playing in clubs. It came in about 2005, and SEAL-TITE had grown to about a $200,000-a-year operation. I was taking home about $50,000 of that, and realized I could survive on it. I thought, "Free weekends! What a great concept." Today, the business does about $750,000 a year, and I have been able to purchase a home, put some retirement money away, and help my children when they need it. It makes me feel good that I took $300 of pocket money, gambled, and built it into a three-quarters of a million dollar annual retail business. I don't feel *proud*, so much, as *thankful* that my days of rolling quarters for gas money and being broke all the time have disappeared. I am grateful, more than anything, because I live in a country where such things are possible. The U.S. is a relatively rich economy on the global front, and the relative stability of our governmental institutions provides laws, roads, communication infrastructure, and many other things that make this a much better place to do business than many other places in the world. We have a growing problem of income inequality, of course, but I'm hoping that, with time, these inequities will start to be addressed.

I only relay this brief history of my business building to clarify how I was able to once-and-for-all step off that very volatile land mine of being forced to play the lounge circuit for a living. Of course, I know a few musicians for whom this lifestyle was not as much of a danger to their sanity and physical well-being as it was for me, but for the majority of them it was. Some of them died as a result of it, many of them found other, less dangerous work, and a scant few are still employed in it today. I still play out in public once in a while, but only a handful of times each year, and only in venues in which I feel comfortable.

Chapter Thirteen
BREAKING THE CHAINS OF RELIGIOUS DOGMA, FINALLY

During the 1980s and 1990s I was busy trying to find my place in life, generate enough money to pay for rent, food, a vehicle, my daughter and son, and other things that responsible people are expected to pay for. I was still reading and thinking because that is an inescapable part of my inherent nature, but the busy-ness and craziness kept me from evolving my thoughts very rapidly. I guess you could say that I still had a core religious belief in Christianity, but it was sort of murky and confused. I was no fundamentalist, as before; but I sort of hung on to a belief that Christianity was generally divine in its origin, and therefore true.

And even though I had rejected the notion that the Bible was "the inerrant word of God," and that much of how Christianity manifests itself in society is bogus, I still had some nagging doubts about the core issue of what happens to us when we die. Was I really sure there is no Hell? Does Heaven exist? Do we really continue to be alive in some conscious form after our tickers stop ticking?

These questions were still plaguing me to some degree; and, in fact, they began to *annoy* me in a sense. I was annoyed, because these issues had followed me through most of my life and had caused me some considerable anxiety. I had stepped on the land mine of conservative Christianity at age 19, and here I was in my forties still suffering psychological injury from it. So, with my new-found available time after I quit working two jobs, I began to focus on trying to discover some answers.

One of the first books I read in the 2000s was Bishop Spong's "Rescuing The Bible From Fundamentalism." In it he expressed with great clarity some of the conclusions I had already reached, but without as much clarity. He spent a fair amount of time clearly explaining how the Bible had come into existence, and that fundamentalists and evangelicals were quite wrong about how they were peddling it. For him, biblical literalism—and hence evangelical doctrine and teaching—are more likely an impediment to the survival of the Church than an impetus to its growth. Dr. Spong believes that there is a kind of post-enlightenment way of salvaging Christianity, which rejects the age-old dogmas about the divinity of Christ, the existence of Hell, and pretty much most of those kinds of doctrines. And he maintains that there is another way to look at it, and that we should look at it that way if Christianity is to survive through the 21st Century. His focal teaching about how we should view it comes in the reputed words of Jesus when he said, "I have come that you might have life, and have it more abundantly" (John 10:10). In other words, for Dr. Spong, the Christian message was designed to be a positive one, one in which a more fulfilling and meaningful life can be had through interaction with the church and communion with God. In taking this position, he is pretty squarely in the camp of what has come to be designated as "neo-Orthodoxy."

In short, he believes that Christianity is real and divine, but that the traditional Christian beliefs—e.g., God created the world in six days, there was a global flood, the earth is about six thousand years old, Adam and Eve were real people, and Jesus was physically resurrected from the dead—are all ancient Bronze Age myths that have no basis in historical fact. They're "bogus," so to speak. But, nonetheless, he reiterates time and again, Christianity is still real and Jesus is still to be listened to and followed.

As I read his words, I found myself pretty drawn to them. I thought, "Here's a way I can accept what I believe are scientific truths about the origin of the world and of man, but can still have some sort of Christian faith." I thus wouldn't have to "throw the baby out with the bathwater," so to speak. But as I thought further, it occurred to me that such a thesis is completely ridiculous. What he is saying—although I doubt he would agree he was saying it—is that the book that all orthodox Christianity claims to have as its basis for belief and practice is pre-scientific and flawed, but you can still believe in some form of the faith itself. For me there is no way to concede that the Bible is full of all kinds of non-historical myths and contradictions, but that the faith it has engendered is still true and valid.

And my intense study of the Old Testament at Wisconsin backed me up in my conclusion. There is nothing even remotely Christian in anything of the books of the Old Testament, and the only reason anybody believes that is because the New Testament authors pulled various passages out of the OT books and declared that they prophetically spoke of the Jesus of Nazareth in 1st Century Palestine. The New Testament authors were thus looking for "proof texts" to support their claim that Jesus was the expected Messiah that the Old Testament books had hinted at in various places. But in so doing, these authors absolutely butchered the clear and historically relevant meaning of the Old Testament passages in question.

As the 2000s continued, I still was searching for how to come to a final conclusion about what I thought about Christianity. And I read three books which helped me sort my thoughts on the matter once and for all. The first was "god is not Great: How Religion Poisons Everything" by Christopher Hitchens, and then "Misquoting Jesus: The Story Behind Who Changed The Bible and Why" by Bart Ehrman, followed by another book of his entitled "Jesus, Interrupted: Revealing The Hidden Contradictions in the Bible." This last book, I think, is the best treatment

I've seen to date of why the many differing views of Christianity should be rejected. And like me, Ehrman was a former evangelical Christian who had once believed in the inerrancy of Scripture.

Other books helpful to my final clarification process were by either ex-evangelicals or atheists, including "Losing Faith in Faith: From Preacher to Atheist" by Dan Barker, who was an evangelical preacher and is now an atheist; books by John Loftus such as "Why I Rejected Christianity: A Former Apologist Explains;" books and articles by evolutionary biologist Richard Dawkins; and other various books and writings by Daniel Dennett and Sam Harris. It seems that in the last decade and a half lots of former evangelicals and fundamentalists are coming out of the woodwork and sharing their departure from the faith in the form of books, articles, interviews, and lectures. I count myself among their number, but without the notoriety. And that's fine with me, because, while I don't blatantly broadcast my agnosticism in my corner of the world here, my honesty about it when asked still causes some ostracization from people that I know.

Today, I would define my position towards—or rather my understanding of—religion in general as follows:

All religions, including Christianity, have some sort of religious texts associated with them. These texts are central to the claims and doctrines advocated by these religions, and they were all produced by men or women who were expressing their views about the divine, the world, and man in their own historical and cultural context. There is no evidence, whatsoever, that any of them has a divine sanction or origin, or has any credibility whatsoever about what may or may not lie behind the observable, physical world. In the case of The Bible, there are hundreds of internal inconsistencies, both historical and theological; and it is at odds in numerous places with what is known from provable science. It is a collection of books written over a period of about one thousand years, by many different authors who had many different viewpoints; and most of it tries to deal with the essential questions that all conscious humans have had since they had the cranial capacity to ponder their surroundings: Where did it all begin? Who is the true divinity and what is his/her/its nature? Why do bad things happen to us? Why do we suffer? What happens after death? What is the proper way of living life? And other related queries.

Given those truths, I have come to regard myself as an *agnostic*, rather than an *atheist*. That is, I am not prepared to categorically deny that there is a divinity, or something approaching that, but a careful analysis of all claims of "holy" books or "holy" men has led me to the conclusion that *none* of them are legitimate or true. In other words, I know what is NOT true; but much of what may be true I don't have the first inkling about. I trust science in its general agreed-upon conclusions (e.g, the origin of the universe and of man, the age of the Earth, natural law, etc.); but the state of scientific knowledge is young compared to what it will be in, say 100 or 1000 years. If some divinity were to show up and clearly make pronouncements about anything at all, I am more than willing to listen. Or if some greatly advanced alien civilization shows up and tells us a whole lot more than we know now, I'll be in the front row with a pen and a notebook.

So the first decade of the 21st century was a defining moment for my religious views. I finally shrugged off the nagging suspicion that Christianity is in *any* sense true, and fully accepted that fear of Hell or an angry god is a waste of time and emotion. There is no formal reality of sin (although bad and immoral behavior is quite real), we have no idea what (if anything) happens after death, and religion is a major factor in why mankind is continually warring with itself. It has its positive consequences, to be sure; and I want to elaborate on that shortly. But none of it is *true*.

To put my historical experience with Christianity succinctly, I would direct your attention to a lyric from Laura Nyro's stellar song (*Goin' Down the*) *Stoney End:* "I was raised on the good book Jesus, 'til I read between the lines."

Chapter Fourteen
WATCH OUT FOR ROMANCE!!!!

The suggestion in the title of this chapter is absurd on its face, of course, because there are few people of any age who would adhere to such a principle. There are indeed some who have "sworn off" ever again getting back on the "fall-in-love train," for various reasons: Perhaps their soul mate for life has passed away, and they feel no one could ever take his or her place. Maybe they've had such a bad experience with the romantic relationship thing that they have vowed never again to open up to another person on that level. Others may be in marriages in which the romance light has long since gone out, but they are resigned to stay in them, even if it means saying good-bye to ever being "in love" again. And some, it seems, just don't feel a need for that aspect of human interaction, so they don't pursue it. I totally get it, and of course everyone's path is his/hers to choose. But I think a majority of unattached people are open to the idea of engaging in a romantic relationship with another person if the opportunity were to present itself.

As for myself, I'm still looking for "her"—my soul mate, my princess, my significant other, my "*it* girl"— even at this relatively late date in my earthly sojourn. I can count the number of women on one hand throughout my life with whom I've been "in love"—three, to be exact— and their names are Renee, LeAnne, and Emlyn.

Now, I have had various kinds of relationships with hundreds of women over the last fifty years: I've had good friends, good "friends with benefits," and women in whom I was romantically interested, but who did not feel the same way about me. Likewise, I've been pursued by a number of women in whom I was not interested. My story is probably not that uncommon. But here are my stories about them, told as honestly as I can tell them, and with the purpose of showing just how "land-miney" romantic relationships can be.

Renee

Although I had engaged in several romantic dalliances and infatuations from age thirteen to age thirty, they were mostly superficial and not really destructive enough in the end to be classified as land mines. Some were "puppy love," some were obsessions, and some were just expressions of raw hormonal responses. But the first real explosive-in-the-end relationship I had was with Renee, a youthful brunette bar patron I met at one of our club gigs.

And each of the three times I did meet a woman who was to become a land mine for me, there were warning signals from the get-go—warning signals that I completely ignored. For example, in the case of Renee, she was nineteen and I was thirty-two. She was pretty, bright, and funny, but simple-minded in her approach to life. She wasn't a bad person, but there really was very little between us that was a foundation upon which to build a deep relationship. We met in one of the several Ramada Inn Lounges that I played during my music career, and the scenario was common: As musicians, we would take a break every hour; and we would often go out into the crowd and mingle with the patrons. I was always "monitoring" the women who would come into the club, and on break I would sometimes approach one of them and ask if they had any requests for songs. One night—a Wednesday, I think—Renee had returned to the Ramada with a female friend to hear us play. On our first break I went over to her table and introduced myself, asking if there was any particular song they'd like to request. She said, "No, just play what you're playing. We like it." I said, "Great, we will," and I reached out my hand to shake hers as I left. "Unh-unh," she objected, "a hand shake ain't gonna get it." And she grabbed the back of my neck and pulled me down to kiss her! I was quite pleased, of course, as I was very attracted to her. Long story short, she began showing up regularly at that Ramada; and, before long, we were living together. I was somewhat conflicted during our days of living in my apartment, 'cause, while I cared about her and enjoyed the company, I never thought that we were in it for the long term. It was this feeling that eventually led me to retreat a bit from her emotionally, plus she was hammering me about getting married. So one day I talked to her and said I thought it might be good if we didn't live together any more. She was hurt, of course; but I think she had seen it coming. At any rate, she moved out, and immediately began dating one of the sax players with the band "The Swinging Medallions." (Remember their hit, "Double Shot of My Baby's Love?").

And then it hit me!!! She was gone! And I wasn't feeling at all good about it!!!! Boy, was there ever a time when the phrase "You don't know what ya got 'til it's gone" applied! So I called her several times and tried to rekindle our relationship, but she wasn't having it. Her new beau was giving her everything she needed—the excitement of the music scene, companionship, sex, etc. And I felt wounded for at least a couple of years after that. During those years, I hit the bottle pretty well, and lost myself in the tawdriest of physical relationships with dozens of women.

LeAnne

At the tail end of my period of grieving over Renee, I met LeAnne, the second of my romantic land mines from whom I had to recover. The scenario was reminiscent of how I had met Renee. We were playing at

Hogan's, the all-night club I previously mentioned. Our guitar player had some interest in her, and she was there to see him. She was sitting at a table near the dance floor, and when I spied her I was blown away. She was pretty, smiling at me (I think), and as I passed by her table walking towards the stage I turned in her direction and said something totally out of The Twilight Zone: "You affect me." Uh, do whaaaaattttt?????!!!!!! "You affect me?????!!!" What a bizarre and totally off-the-wall thing to say to someone you haven't even met yet! But she seemed to understand what I was saying; and, long story short, we began seeing each other.

This went on for a few months, but our problem was very much the same as the one I had with Renee. LeAnne was nineteen, and I was thirty-five, and we didn't have an awful lot to talk about after the first month of dating. So we both became increasingly aloof emotionally, and we went our separate ways. But we never formally "broke up," and four or five years later I invited her to my 20th high school reunion. She said yes, and we had a fairly good time; but that old flame was rekindled in me and I wanted to jump back into our relationship with both feet. She didn't feel the same way, however, so another five years or so passed and we had no interaction.

However, somewhere close to 1995, she called me, while I was living with a woman named Cheryl, who was to later become my second wife. (I met Cheryl at The Mountain Brook Inn, another club I was playing at in the early 90s. I ended up moving in with her and marrying her, as I earlier said primarily because my daughter *loved* her. (But also because she was Canadian, didn't have a green card, and she was catching a little heat from the immigration authorities). And when I told LeAnne I was about to get married to Cheryl, she seemed a little disturbed at the notion. This caught me by surprise, and I registered it in my mind. In fact, when I told her I was about to walk the aisle in a month, she blurted out, "Oh really? So am I." And not long after, she did. However, the guy she married was from Washington state, and she ended up moving there and having two sons with him.

Fast forward to 2008, nearly 13 years after I had last spoken with her, and I was about to squarely step on what was probably the biggest romantic land mine of my life. From time to time I had thought about her over those years, and I wondered what and how she was doing. Since I was fully into the Internet thing by that time, I began to search for her in various places online. One day, I discovered MySpace, one of the earliest Facebook-type social media sites; and I typed in her name. And *voila!!!!*—there she was! So I messaged her; and, lo and behold, she called me from Washington. Turns out she had just divorced her husband and was sort of dating some guy she'd recently met. But she seemed very happy to talk to me, and not twenty-four hours later I got a call from her at about 10 o'clock at night. She was crying, and explained that she was in her car and had just left her guy friend's house because he had called it quits with her. Now, I was already interested in exploring if she and I might rekindle our relationship, and I was so lonely at the time that I was more than ready to open up and take the full plunge into "Loveland." So I listened attentively as she drove home; and, long story short, we began talking on the phone every day for the next month.

During that time, she had called me from a club she was at one Friday night; and she said, "Wait a sec, I'm gonna go outside so I can tell you something." When she got outside, she said, "Jim, I think I love you. No, no, I don't think so, I do." I responded with, "Well, Leanne, I adore you, too." I didn't want to use the "L" word until I could tell her face to face, 'cause I wanted her to be able to look at me and know the sincerity of my feelings for her. So, after that initial month, I flew her to Birmingham one weekend; and we spent a Saturday together. We attended a friend of mine's daughter's wedding in Huntsville and had a fantastic time. But there was something nagging at me about some of her responses to me. She seemed to be in love with me, and I told her I wanted to marry her and grow old together; but there was a hesitation in some of her responses. I look back now and think that she knew our respective living situations might present a problem for us. Since she had two sons, she was not allowed by law to take them out of state. And I was knee-deep in my business and not yet wealthy enough to up and move to Washington. But we continued to talk on the phone for a couple of weeks after that. I had reverted back into some fairly heavy drinking during those two weeks because this relationship was scaring the shit out of me.

And then, as quickly as it heated up, it crashed and burned. She realized I couldn't come to her, and I knew she couldn't come to me; and she bailed on us early one Saturday morning. I didn't feel too badly about it on that day; but, as the days passed and I got more sober, it started to hurt pretty bad. It made me physically sick for about a week, and I had trouble eating and sleeping. I monitored her Facebook page during those days, torturing myself with each log in to see what she was doing. Evidently, she was not nearly as broke up as I was about our split; and, in fact, within a couple of months, she had found a new beau for herself. And in less than a year she married him, once and for all closing the saga of Jim and LeAnne. (At least I think that's the case).

As I reflect on that short two-month disaster, I recall one day in which I felt something for her that I had never felt as strongly before with anyone. She called me as I was driving to Memphis—this being before she had come to visit me in Birmingham—and as I talked with her, I felt this explosion of romantic love inside of me. It engulfed my whole being, and I was floating in another plane of existence. "This is the real deal," I told myself, and I still haven't changed my opinion about that. I hope one day to experience that once again, but who knows what life will bring?

Emlyn

The third, and final romantic land mine I stepped on was with a girl I met in 1990. Chronologically, she was the second in the trio of explosive romantic disasters I've had; but I had actually met LeAnne before I met her, and I wanted to tell the LeAnne story in a single narrative. Number three's name was Emlyn; and, just like before, I met her in a Ramada Inn where we were playing. (In fact, it was the same Ramada Inn where I had met Renee years before). I don't recall the specifics of our first encounter, but she was an accomplished woman much closer to my age. I was thirty-eight, and she was about thirty-four. She was from Cincinnati, and had taken a job in Birmingham due to the fact that she had recently separated from her husband in Ohio. At any rate she took a sincere liking to me, and I to her. She was a professional woman, self-sufficient, pretty, funny; and we hit it off right away. She traveled a lot with her job; but at least a couple of nights a week she would come into the Ramada, and I would sometimes end up staying the night with her. We talked on the phone a lot, and at some point I felt like I had fallen in love with her. We talked about maybe marrying over the period of about the next year, and I was open to the idea.

But during that time I began to see some things in her that I didn't care for, one being that without provocation she was occasionally rude or ugly to people we would encounter. She once told a male waiter in a restaurant where we were eating that it was "pretty presumptuous" of him to hand the dinner check to me, and that he needed to get on board with the equal status of women in the 1990s. This poor guy was probably nineteen, maybe working his way through school by waiting tables, and I saw no reason for her to be so caustic with him (even if she had a point). I also heard a rumor or two that she had slept with another guy or two while we were ostensibly in an exclusive relationship, and I didn't know quite what to make of that. At any rate, I was pretty deep into the relationship emotionally; and I ignored the things about her that put me off.

However, after being in Ohio for Christmas 1991, she returned back to Birmingham on the 26th of December and announced to me that she was considering going back to her husband. (Let me tell ya, that rained shit on that particular Christmas for me, and it screwed up a bunch of my Christmases in the years after that!). I tried to hang onto her for a couple of months after that announcement, but one day she just up and left. And that sent me into a slough of despair for a couple of years after that. What kind of an asshole dumps a boyfriend or girlfriend right at Christmas? And there it was, that familiar pain I had experienced from unrequited love in previous years. But as time ticked on, I got over it; and, when I had enough distance from it, I realized what a self-interested person she was. And how I had dodged a bullet with her.

The Lesson Learned

After all this emotional drama over the span of about five decades, I think I have finally diagnosed the problem I've had in these relationships: *My heart jumped in with little or no oversight from my head.* I'm sure that's a pretty common occurrence, and romantic relationships are fraught with risk in many cases. But we are social creatures, and most of us need the emotional intimacy of a close relationship with another human being.

I find it amusing that it took me nearly half a century to learn how to guard my romantic inclinations until my head could properly evaluate the situation, but a recent relationship has convinced me that I'm pretty much there. This happened when I took up with a girl about 25 years my junior (a familiar scenario, huh?), a girl who has lots of very pleasant qualities: she's pretty kind, she's funny, she's pretty, she's smart, and she's very self-sufficient. We were even talking marriage at one point, but I held off until I could have a couple of very deep conversations with her about what she wanted out of life. Once I did that, and got her very honest answers, I knew that we could never be a "forever" pair. We weren't right for each other, even though she remains a good friend to this day. And as if to confirm my evaluation of the situation, she recently up and married another guy. I wasn't her Romeo, and she wasn't my Juliet; and we are both better for having determined that before we did something stupid.

Now, I realize that pontificating about romance is a risky business in itself, cause romance is probably the one thing that is not totally controllable by any human being. But I feel pretty certain that I have stepped on my last romantic mine in the minefield of life. However, I'm still waiting on "her," and I'm emotionally and mentally better positioned than ever to make that happen.

Chapter Fifteen
BEWARE THE BOOZE MINE!!!

People drink or self-medicate for a lot of different reasons. Some are able to do it without being abusive to themselves, and some aren't. I was one of those who let the regimen of regular boozing go to extremes at times.

Perhaps one of the most common reasons people drink is that alcohol relieves stress (temporarily). It also relieves emotional pain (also temporarily). It can also drag one out of depression (*very* temporarily) while simultaneously dragging one into depression. (Alcohol is a depressant).

Some folks have a drink or two after work to counter the "stress" of the day. Some folks drink because there is some fundamental uneasiness in their lives, such as poor economic status, loss of a child or a loved one, romantic rejection, low self-esteem, being the victim of emotional or physical abuse, general fear about the future, being in a stressful relationship, a desire to "escape" the real world for any number of reasons, or just about anything that can come with being a sojourner on earth. In fact, at this very second, it is estimated that between one and five million Americans are *drunk*. And a great many more are physically and mentally altered from either legal or illegal drug use.

And, believe me, I get it. Alcohol and drugs perform a myriad of "helpful" things to people who are hurting or stressing. The problem is, of course, that no drug (and alcohol *is* a drug) can address the root problems or circumstances that cause us to self-medicate. Once the mind-numbing wears off from ingesting a substance, the problem is still there. And if you physically feel bad after a booze or drug bender, it makes those problems seem even larger and more difficult to cope with than before you got drunk or drugged up.

My own experience with alcohol abuse was a little less driven by my desire to escape internal pain or external stress, but at times those factors did affect my overuse of it.

Early Forays into the "Demon Rum"

I have already described (in Chapter 3) my first excursion into getting drunk. I was about thirteen, and the experience was not a particularly pleasant one. But I was running with a crowd in junior high that revered alcohol as something that was "cool" and "hip." It was *party fuel*, and my running buddies were all constantly scheming to get their hands on beer, wine, or hard liquor, even though we were well below the legal drinking age.

I would say that my evolution into more regular drinking was spurred mostly from a desire to party and feel good, rather than a desire to escape anything. As I got older, my access to booze increased; and, by the time I was eighteen, I was drinking beer or attending a drinking party somewhere almost every weekend. As I've said before, my goals at this point in life were mostly partying, trying to get laid, and searching for romance. And in these early days my physical and mental experience with booze was a euphoric one—i.e., getting "high" felt *really* good, and transformed me into another realm that was sort of magical. I imagine that this was why I gravitated much more to alcohol than to pot or pill-form drugs. I just really liked the sensation of hooch better than that of other drugs.

My Evolution into A Different Kind of Drinking

Up until age nineteen, my drinking habits were not really pronounced in the way that they later became. I would never "binge drink" (in the sense that I would drink for several days non-stop), and my drinking was mostly confined to weekends or "party" times.

And when I was "born again" into Christian fundamentalism at age 19, my boozing completely stopped for several years. In fact, I didn't really do any serious drinking for about a ten-year stretch (which encompassed my twenties). However, over that ten-year period, my adherence to fundamentalist religion was slowly beginning to erode; and the fundamentalist "taboo" I felt about drinking began to erode with it.

I first began to drink pretty regularly when I returned to Birmingham in 1981 and eventually became a musician on the nightclub circuit. The nightclub circuit involved playing in a bar five to seven nights every week, and this went on for about twenty years. (With only about six total weeks off during those twenty years!!!). And let me tell you, drinking was front-and-center in those bars. Almost every one of them was a party-type bar, where people didn't come to sip Courvoisier and ponder Kant. They came, *en masse*, to drink heavily and hook-up with a partner. Drinking-and-screwing was the order of the day, and I jumped right in.

For the first ten years or so of my musical career, I confined some pretty serious drinking to the nighttime performance hours. I could get buzzed, and even drunk for the last song set, and there was no problem. The next-day hangover was pretty routine; but, with plenty of good food and a shower later, I was right back into the nightly party and drinking routine again. In fact, as the years passed and the novelty of playing on stage began to wear off, I found myself drinking just to get through the night. Many people think playing music in a bar band is easy, and just one big never-ending party. It isn't, particularly if you're a serious musician who brings 100% every night to the performance. And I was (and am) that type of musician. Having that much emotional outflow nearly every night of the week over a couple of decades begins to drain you emotionally and psychologically, not to mention what the late hours do to you physically. And drinking helps to mitigate those problems as well as enable you to maintain some sense of enjoyment about it all.

The Worst Times

I could write a book ten times as long as this one about the booze-related experiences I had in the 80s and 90s (and some into the New Millennium), but I'll spare you all the gory details. Suffice it to say that there was puking behind the speaker stack stage left, playing with the shakes after coming off of a three-day bender (excruciatingly painful with the drums pounding in my ear), crying while singing some pretty ballad, once falling off my chair in the middle of a song (my bandmates were already lying down onstage, still playing), once walking out of the club after the first set and not coming back, forgetting lyrics I had sung one hundred times before, and more. These events were rare, but they still happened. And not only that, but excessive drinking led me to countless after-hours trysts with women that I had absolutely nothing in common with (except a desire to "knock boots"). It's astonishing to me that I avoided both herpes and the HIV virus after these innumerable exploits. (And yes, I've been medically checked quite a number of times).

Stepping off The Booze Landmine

During those years of abusive drinking I would sometimes stop for a week or two, but prolonged exposure to that party culture eventually led me back in. It was not until about ten years ago that I more or less stopped drinking as a routine behavior, and I didn't do it on any given date. It was more of an evolving process, probably spurred by several facts: Hangovers hurt more than they used to (tip of the cap to Hank Williams, Jr.), my economic status greatly improved the less I drank, I became focused on certain goals I wanted to accomplish (relating to business, recording music, and writing), and, most importantly, I quit playing music for a living. If I were to be forced back into having to play music every night of the week on the club circuit, I'm pretty certain that I'd end up having to drink my way through it again. Fortunately, I'm in a financial position that all but guarantees that'll never be the case again. Don't get me wrong, I still play publicly maybe three to four times a year, but that's about it.

How To Step Off

I believe there are many ways to defeat an addiction to or dependence on anything, including alcohol or drugs. The first step, obviously, is to recognize that you have a problem (if you do). You can't set out to change a destructive behavior unless you believe you have that behavior.

The next step would be to try and evaluate *why* you are drinking or drugging to excess (if you are). You may need the external help of a therapist or psychiatrist (though good ones are sometimes hard to find), or you may be able to discover the reason yourself. But dealing with the underlying cause of an addiction is *paramount* in my view. People don't drink or abuse drugs because they are morally weak or somehow ethically inferior, they do it *for a reason*. And discovering that reason is critical to defeating the need to abuse.

In my own case, I think my life circumstances had a little bit to do with why I drank: low self-esteem, being broke half the time, and the fact that I was genetically predisposed to enjoy being buzzed. But my chosen occupation as a lounge musician was the main reason. I can't be in a party atmosphere every night, where most people are drunk by 11 PM, and not be obliged to join them in the festivities. Also, being around drunk people when I'm 100% sober is highly annoying to me. And putting out that kind of emotional performance night after night after night is too draining on me without drinking. So, I chose a different line of work that removed me from that environment, and an immediate decline in my drinking habits followed.

I realize that my former attachment to alcohol may be a little different than that of some folks. Everyone has their own reasons for drug dependence, and those reasons are sometimes complex. But if you have a problem, I would suggest that you focus on trying to find your own pathway out of it.

I am not a big fan of AA (or NA), mainly because their own studies show that their success rate is about 5%. That means that 95 out of every 100 people who enter a program like that don't solve their problem—and that's a pretty terrible track record. There are many other things about AA that I fundamentally disagree with, ranging from their philosophy that you must admit you are powerless against alcohol, that you must submit to a "higher power," and that you have a "disease" that never goes away. Perhaps these defeatist principles are part of the reason their success rate is so low, but who knows. If you are part of the lucky 5% for whom AA works, more power to you! I don't care what program or philosophy or path you choose to free yourself, if it gets you where you want to be, then wonderful! But over the past twenty years or so new substance abuse programs that are more empowering and focused on root causes have emerged in large number, and their success rates are much higher.

So whatever you can do to seek out help to deal with your addiction, do it! You're not powerless, you don't have an incurable disease, and you don't need to passively submit to a "higher power" to break the chains of your dependence. But take it seriously, cause addictions can, and do, *kill*.

I can name at least a dozen fellow musicians or bar staff I knew who died from liver cirrhosis, kidney failure, strokes, or other alcohol-related diseases. And addictions can cause endless amounts of misery not only to you, but to those around you. In America, more than 88,000 people die every year from alcohol, and about 15 million have some sort of "alcohol use disorder." 65 million report binge drinking within the last month, and all these numbers have been on the upswing over the past ten years. On the drug front, the numbers are equally alarming. More than 72,000 die each year from drug overdoses, and it's estimated that 20 million Americans have a "drug use disorder." These numbers are also increasing.

For me personally, I just made a decision over time that I was tired of physically feeling like shit, tired of the guilt, depression, and anxiety that the chemical substances in alcohol were causing in my life, and I was tired of causing anxiety to those in my life whom I truly love. It was not a religiously *moral* decision; it was simply a common-sense decision. And the sober life, while not a perfect one, is a *much* happier life than the chemically dependent one. And as a bonus, it also leads to a better life economically. I estimate that over the past 3 decades I've lost about $200,000 due to the various costs associated with drinking—the cost of the booze itself, lost business profits because I was drinking and not focusing, and the cost of a couple of DUIs. Hey, $200,000 will buy a nice house in many cities these days.

I didn't attend AA or go to rehab (which is often more about playing ping pong and having group meetings for a ridiculously high price)—I just *quit,* without obsessing over the issue 24/7. Some folks will, of course, absolutely *have to* go into a rehab or detox center just to get free of the immediate danger they are in from prolonged drinking or drugging (by going through medically monitored detox and being physically separated from alcohol or drugs. Don't try and do it on your own, because seizures and other dangerous physical effects can occur). But if you do choose the longer-term rehab route, I'd suggest finding a modern one that is not tied to AA. If that's all that's available in your area or within your budget, then that's fine. But do *something*. You possess infinite value, and *you don't have to live like that!!*

In short, I stepped on the land mine of frequent boozing, *and I survived it.* And so can you!!!

Chapter Sixteen
WATCH OUT FOR THE RELIGION MINE!!!

I have chronicled my experience into, and out of, religion in the previous pages. I'd like to now generalize about it in a broader way.

People appropriate religion into their lives in many different ways and for many different reasons. In Western culture the dominant religion is Christianity. In Eastern culture Islam and Hinduism are dominant. (Buddhism isn't properly a *religion* in most of its various forms, but it is dominant in many countries).

One of the ways we here in the West end up believing in a certain form of religion is because we are taught it from a very early age. Our parents take us to church, where a particular brand of Christianity is hammered into us during our formative years. It is reinforced at home by our parents; and, by the time we gain the intellectual ability to critically think for ourselves, we are already knee-deep into whatever Christian brand we were born into.

Perhaps you were raised Catholic. Perhaps Protestant. And within these two broad categories you may have been indoctrinated into either fundamentalist (evangelical) or liberal types of the religion. And within those categories, you may be Pentecostal/Methodist/Baptist/Presbyterian/Independent Bible Church (popular today)/Lutheran/Presbyterian/etc., or Traditional/Orthodox/Progressive Catholic. Or you may have been raised in the Eastern Orthodox Christian traditions. And that is not an exhaustive list, by any means. And most of these "brands" of

Christianity are *not* compatible with each other. Think of that for a minute. The chance that you were brought up in the *one* correct version (among hundreds) of one of the many major religions across the globe—due to where you were born—is highly improbable and statistically absurd.

The point is, *there is no such thing as a "single" Christianity*. It would be more accurate to talk about "Christianities." And even *within* a single type or brand of Christianity, there are differences of doctrinal beliefs among its individual adherents in any given church. For example, not every member of The First Baptist Church on the corner has exactly the same beliefs about every single religious doctrine or practice. In my own evangelical church, there were frequent arguments about such things as a believer's "election" by God, to what degree "predestination" was a reality, whether abortion in the case of familial rape was OK, whether divorce was ever acceptable, whether women could be pastors, and a bunch of other nonsense.

And the same is true in other religions—e.g., there are Sunni and Shiite Muslims, Vaishnav and Shaiv Hindus (and dozens of subsects of each), and etc. And in Buddhism there are so many different sects that modern scholars are hesitant to concede that you can even talk about such a thing as "Buddhism" as a definable single entity. (And again, Buddhism is not really a religion in the usual sense). In short, religious belief is a hodge-podge of traditions and opinions, and one needs to be careful about generalizing about what "Christians, Muslims, Hindus, Buddhists, etc. etc. etc." *believe*. They believe a lot of different things, and they behave accordingly.

Why People Are Religious

As to why humans appropriate religion in general, one can say that there are many reasons. Religion provides many benefits to an individual's life and emotional well-being. The human experience is fraught with difficulties and traumas, and religion is one way to cope with them.

Perhaps the most common is the need to deal with death. Most Christians, of whatever stripe, believe that life continues after death, and that the people we lose have not been lost forever. This need to mitigate the pain of a loved one's loss is quite understandable, and the idea that we'll one day see Mom or Dad or Grandma or Grandpa or a lost child or lover in Paradise is more than comforting. However, that same belief in an afterlife can also be traumatizing, as it was to me concerning my dad's death. When he died, I was not an evangelical; but, years later, I accepted the belief that unless a person was "born again," that person was forever burning in Hell after death. My dad had never made mention of any born-again experience, and the anxiety level I experienced in thinking he was agonizing in the flames of Hell fucked up my mind for many years. You see, I took my evangelical beliefs very seriously.

Another reason people appropriate religion is the need to make sense of life's circumstances. The loss of a job, financial security, a friend, a lover, a pet, a home, a car, a career, a bodily limb, a litigation, one's health, or a parking spot can provide anxiety or fear or pain on a grand level. But those anxieties and pains are made easier to deal with if one believes that "all things are working together for good" because they are allowed or planned by a loving and sovereign God who is totally in control of it all. The notion that these can be alternatively explained by the simple aphorism "shit happens" is a difficult thing to accept. I remember a girlfriend telling me that my philosophy that our earthly life may be random and all that we have was not going to be acceptable in our relationship.

Another reason people appropriate religion in their lives has to do with finding a sense of personal purpose. The idea that we may have appeared upon the scene in space and time by a random evolutionary process, and that there is no "plan" or "purpose" except that which we assign for ourselves, is not easy to accept. It's much easier to navigate life if we believe that we are being monitored and guided by a benevolent deity, and that this omniscient being has a step-by-step plan he has laid out for us individually. It gives us a sense of worth, and that there is nothing that happens that is random. "God loves you, and has a wonderful plan for your life" is the way Bill Bright's "Four Spiritual Laws" tract put it.

Another common reason why people inculcate religion into their lives has to do with the need to absolve a sense of guilt they have developed over what they perceive as their past sins or mistakes. I myself had this as one motivating factor, because at age nineteen I'd broken just about every one of the commandments on God's "Top Ten" list. I felt guilty and looked at myself as a "sinner" who needed to "get right with God." And when I transferred that guilt over to what I thought was God's merciful offer of salvation, I experienced a certain peace in my life. My sense of guilt was lifted, and I could sleep better at night. Of course, that whole perception of guilt was the result of cultural conditioning—i.e., I was conditioned by my upbringing to think of myself as a sinner, then conditioned to accept forgiveness from a made-up deity. My experience was real, but there was no underlying reality in fact. There was no "sin" to begin with, and there was no god "forgiving me" at that point in time. Getting drunk, cursing, and having premarital sex with different women can be unwise in some cases, but it is not "sin."

I must also point out that when it comes to how people appropriate religion and religious doctrine into their lives, it's often the case that they do it based on whatever suits their personal experience the best. Most people aren't going to adopt a belief system that makes them feel bad or anxious. They're going to take whatever general religious tradition they accept and then modify the particulars to meet their unique emotional and psychological needs. For example, if you need to punt all personal responsibility for your particular lot in life, you are likely to appropriate a strong belief in the predestination and sovereignty of God: "He's calling the shots, and I'm just a passive vessel in His Divine plan." Or alternatively, if you have a pretty high opinion of your performance in life, you may adopt a more "Methodist" view of the Divine: "God helps those who help themselves." Sociologists, anthropologists, and psychologists have penned thousands of pages on the subject of religious appropriation, and I am none of the above. But I have seen it in action over many decades, and *people do indeed adopt whatever form of religion best meets their personal needs, as opposed to adopting what they might have discovered through a sincere and dispassionate search for the truth.*

<u>Why Religion Was A Land Mine for Me</u>

The reason religion was a land mine for me is because I truly believed much of what The Bible says in its various pages. I believed that I am fundamentally a sinner, an offensive person to God, and that my only true worth was that I had been assigned worth by that God when I became a Christian. I believed in "original sin"—the belief that since we are all descendants of Adam, we are desperately wicked in the eyes of God—by birth. This is referred to by theologians as "total depravity." There is something truly psychologically perverse about this idiocy. The notion that humans are fundamentally evil is one of the worst things to come out of the Christian tradition. If taken seriously and personally, it results in a person developing an extremely low self-image, an image that you are fundamentally flawed or evil and that you need a god to tolerate you (through His "grace") for you to have value. I am appalled at this notion these days, after having concluded that Christianity and all its doctrines are not true. (This all has the stench of what psychologists refer to as "Stockholm Syndrome.")

Another reason that Christianity was harmful to me was my belief in the doctrine that all people are going to Hell unless they get "saved." And this Hell is a flaming torture chamber, where people burn FOREVER!!! And I therefore constantly felt a need to ignore my own time and responsibility constraints, and get out there and "save" as many people as I could. After all, NOTHING else in life is comparably important if that is true; and I felt the weight of that idiocy. I also suffered other perverse thoughts--since I believed in The Devil—like, "What if my own salvation is merely a Satanic illusion and I might be instantaneously dispatched off to Hell at any moment!!" I tell you, folks, I really *believed* in the biblical tenets of Christianity, and it was more than unsettling in many ways.

There are many other experiential reasons that Christianity was harmful to me—because I believed in the "biblical" view of it—and I'll just mention a couple here without elaborating. The Bible constantly talks about the evils of physical lust, and, boy, was I "wired for sound" on that front! In my twenties and thirties, I was a real horned dog, and I constantly felt that my sexual urges were evil. Looking back now, that is of course nonsense, as I was just manifesting how biological evolution had programmed me. Sex is not evil, nor are sexual urges. Another way in which it harmed me was that I was running into walls all the time in trying to salvage my faith in the light of the ever-increasing onslaught of the facts of science. For example, the Bible asserts that the earth is about 6,000 years old (by genealogy trace the birth of Adam on the sixth day to Jesus, which is about 4,000 years, and then from Jesus to now, which is about 2,000 years). Hell, we've got trees that are 80,000 years old, human remains that are 300,000 years old, and a geologic record that puts the earth's age at about 4.5 billion years. I was constantly trying to hold on to my Bible-based faith while simultaneously accepting the various consensuses of science, and it was exhausting. There were other ways in which Christianity was beating me up, but suffice it to say that it was an unnatural and harmful influence.

Now, I know that I was not the typical Christian, because most Christians adopt their beliefs, and adjust them, to make the religion provide a maximum emotional and psychological benefit to them. I was never able to do that, because I have always been a slave to the truth. I will seek out what is empirically, rationally, and demonstrably true to the best of my ability, even if it leads me into places I don't like. I was never one to allow "cognitive dissonance" to reign in my thoughts, because I could never reject what I discovered to be the truth. (Cognitive dissonance is the retention of two contradictory thoughts in your head, which you happily accept as your rational state).

While religion was a stumbling block—or rather a land mine—to me, I also realize that it is *not* for most people. And I have often pondered what a "religion-less world" might look like. The "new atheists" (Hitchens, Dawson, Dennet, Harris, etc.) have discussed this at some length, and I can only see a mixed- bag type of result if such were the case. Many people would be unable to cope with the real traumas of life, and would likely be in rough emotional and psychological shape without it. We all have our mechanisms for coping with life (religion, booze, drugs, work, fantasy, sex, busy-ness, etc.), but I am unable to give assent to anything I know to be untrue. And most religionists don't ever ask the question, "Is my religion true?" because it requires a lot of reading and thinking. And that's not why they adopt religious beliefs to begin with. But, on the other hand, training a child to believe in something that is manifestly an illusion is not a desirable goal, either. It leads to that child becoming an adult who is more prone to believe in other kinds of fantasies and untruths, rather than dealing with reality as it is. And God knows religion has done a huge amount of damage in the world in the form of wars, child abuse, murder, theft, psychological and emotional injury, and etc. So I don't have an answer to this dilemma. As an agnostic, I know that all of the religions being peddled around the world as true are *not* true; but I have no idea whether a superior intellect or being exists. I'm not even sure we have the intellectual capacity to ask the right question about that subject.

If I were to offer advice about how to practice the inevitable religious beliefs that are going to long outlast me and subsequent generations in this world, I would say this: If your religion causes you to do harm to your fellow humans *on any level*, readjust it. If you beat or emotionally abuse your children because they don't conform to your particular code of religious morality, stop it. If you hate or do harm to other people because your holy book says that homosexuality is sin, stop it. It you hate or speak ill of other people because they have different beliefs or a different religion than you do, stop it. If your religion causes you to do things that are irrational, such as withholding medical treatment for a sick family member because you think God is going to heal him or her, stop it. If you practice manifestly unhealthy living traits—like eating or drinking things that medical science has deemed harmful, or by withholding vaccinations from your children for common diseases like measles or polio because you believe that "God is in control, and he has everybody's life span already mapped out," stop it. In short, if your religion causes you to harm others *in any way whatsoever*, STOP IT!!!

For me personally, I am a much happier and (I think) better psychologically adjusted person without believing in something that has no basis in fact. I have studied and pondered Christianity for decades, and I can say that there is no credible evidence that there is some supernatural reality behind it. The Bible, upon which most of Christianity depends for its dogma, is merely a very interesting collection of books that sprung from the Canaanite tribe known as "the Hebrews" in the first and second millennia B.C., and then from the offshoot of Judaism known as Christianity in the first century A.D. Jesus of Nazareth is dead, there is no god by the name of Yahweh, there is no coming Anti-Christ or Armageddon, and your fate is mostly in your hands. I like much of what the biblical books (primarily the Gospels) paint as the history of Jesus, but even this history is manipulated and unreliable in its totality. My favorite teachings of his come in Matthew, chapters 5-8 and chapter 25. He was (allegedly) all about empathetic living and loving your neighbor. Good stuff, by and large.

Not Gonna Step on That Mine Again

Of all the land mines I've stepped on in my life and survived, I can say that religion is the one I'm 100% sure I will *never* step on again. I am about 95% confidant I won't step on the booze landmine again, and about 90% sure I won't step on the landmine of ill-considered romance again. I'm certain the reason I won't get tripped up on religion again is because choosing to *not* believe in any of the existing religions is an intellectual question I settled long ago, and I'm *convinced of the facts*. However, when it comes to stepping on the booze landmine again, that is not quite as much of an intellectual exercise. People drink abusively because they want to alter an uncomfortable reality in their lives, so the decision to do that or not is more of an emotional exercise. But I'm good with being a *very* infrequent drinker, because this primarily sober life is *much* better than the one in which I was drinking all the time. I feel better, emotionally and physically, and I rarely struggle with depression. When it comes to the romance battle—the one that can go on between your heart and your head—I'm pretty certain I won't repeat my former mistakes. But you know how that romance thing goes. Sometimes we get in a little too deep with the heart, and our rational selves begin to malfunction. This is not to say that I'm closed to the possibility of falling in love one last time. It's actually very much the opposite. As I said earlier, I'm still looking for "her," but I think I'm in a much better position now than in earlier times to avoid making a mistake.

At any rate, the religion-less life is for me a liberated one. One which is pervaded by happiness, freedom, and the desire to "do good" while I'm here. I wish the same for you, and I hope my short recounting of my survival from religion will be helpful to you.

Chapter Seventeen
FINAL THOUGHTS

As I've traveled this country and others, I've come to notice one thing: People are the same wherever you go (nod to Paul McCartney and Stevie Wonder). We *all* are emotional beings who need love, acceptance, and a sense of peace in our lives. In our forays down life's road, most of us step on metaphorical mines that injure us to one degree or another. Your mines may or may not be the same or similar to mine. But they are mines just the same.

If you are standing on one as we speak, try and determine what it is and how you came to be standing on it. If you're struggling with an addiction, do a little soul-searching and seek whatever kind of outside help or personal change in mental perception that you need. If you're in a bad romance (only a *half-nod* to Lady Gaga, since she advocated *for* it), try and evaluate what you need to do about it: Leave it? Communicate more with your partner to try and fix it? Get outside help? If you're contemplating romance with someone, do your best to think it through before you get too deep into it. (Tough, I know). If you're involved in a religion that causes you to hate or exclude people who aren't like you, do some investigating to see if what you believe is true. (Spoiler: It *isn't*.) If you *must* have religion in your life because of the overall difficult nature of life—whatever religion it is—try and focus on the positive aspects of its founder's teaching. Jesus reportedly talked a lot about helping the poor, not "returning evil for evil," treating little children with compassion, visiting the incarcerated, not being judgmental, and in general "treating others as you would have them treat you." Islam, in both the Koran and Hadith, advocates showing hospitality and compassion to others. Buddhism and Hinduism have similar tenets, and most of the others do as well.

In short, once you are born into this life, you'll undoubtedly encounter its various (metaphorical) land mines; and you are going to step on a few. But, as Einstein reportedly once said (he didn't really say or write it in so many words, but he certainly implied it), "The definition of insanity is doing the same thing over and over again but expecting different results." In our context, that would mean we should avoid stepping on the same land mines over and over again. Some can prove fatal if repeatedly stepped on, but all are to be avoided as much as possible.

I like to end much of what I write with my adaptation of a sentiment that comes from the main character of the 1960s Broadway play *Mame*: "*Life is a smorgasbord, but most of us poor bastards just stand around at the salad bar.*"

In the context of our discussion, I would alter that to say:

"*Life is a smorgasbord, but beware the land mines as you walk through the serving line!*"

www.ingramcontent.com/pod-product-compliance
Lightning Source LLC
Chambersburg PA
CBHW070614010526
44118CB00012B/1512